Practical Network Automation

Leverage the power of Python and Ansible to optimize your network

Abhishek Ratan

BIRMINGHAM - MUMBAI

Practical Network Automation

First published: November 2017

Production reference: 1141117

Published by Packt Publishing Ltd.
Livery Place
35 Livery Street
Birmingham
B3 2PB, UK.

ISBN 978-1-78829-946-6

www.packtpub.com

Credits

Author
Abhishek Ratan

Reviewer
Pradeeban Kathiravelu

Commissioning Editor
Gebin George

Acquisition Editor
Prateek Bharadwaj

Content Development Editor
Abhishek Jadhav

Technical Editor
Swathy Mohan

Copy Editor
Safis Editing

Project Coordinator
Judie Jose

Proofreader
Safis Editing

Indexer
Pratik Shirodkar

Graphics
Tanya Dutta

Production Coordinator
Melwyn Dsa

About the Author

Abhishek Ratan has around 15 years of technical experience in networking, automation, and various ITIL processes, and has worked in various roles in different organizations. As a network engineer, security engineer, automation engineer, TAC engineer, tech lead, and content writer, he has gained a wealth of experience during the 15 years of his career. Abhishek also has a deep interest in strategy game playing, and if he is not working on technical stuff, he is busy spending time on his strategy games.

He is currently working as a Sr Automation Engineer at ServiceNow, learning, and expanding his automation skills in the ServiceNow platform. His earlier experience includes working for companies such as Microsoft, Symantec, and Navisite,which has given him exposure to various environments.

I would like to give special thanks to the entire editorial team that has helped me throughout this book, from correcting my typo mistakes to making me realize where the flow of content needs to be improved. I would also like to thank my family for being supportive and giving me ample time and support to make this book see the light of the day.

About the Reviewer

Pradeeban Kathiravelu is an open source evangelist. He is a PhD researcher at INESC-ID Lisboa/Instituto Superior Técnico, Universidade de Lisboa, Portugal, and Université Catholique de Louvain, Belgium. He is a fellow of Erasmus Mundus Joint Degree in distributed computing (EMJD-DC), researching a software-defined approach to quality of service and data quality in multi-tenant clouds.

He holds a masters of science degree, Erasmus Mundus European Master in Distributed Computing (EMDC) from Instituto Superior Técnico, Portugal, and KTH Royal Institute of Technology, Sweden. He also holds a first class bachelor of science of engineering (Hons) degree, majoring in computer science and engineering from the University of Moratuwa, Sri Lanka.

His research interests include software-defined networking (SDN), distributed systems, cloud computing, web services, big data in biomedical informatics, and data mining.

He is very interested in free and open source software development and has been an active participant of the Google Summer of Code (GSoC) program since 2009, as a student and mentor.

He has authored *Python Network Programming Cookbook - Second Edition* and has also reviewed two Packt books on OpenDaylight.

I would like to thank Prof. Luís Veiga, my MSc and PhD advisor for his continuous guidance and encouragement throughout my time at Instituto Superior Técnico.

www.PacktPub.com

For support files and downloads related to your book, please visit www.PacktPub.com.

Did you know that Packt offers eBook versions of every book published, with PDF and ePub files available? You can upgrade to the eBook version at www.PacktPub.com and as a print book customer, you are entitled to a discount on the eBook copy. Get in touch with us at service@packtpub.com for more details.

At www.PacktPub.com, you can also read a collection of free technical articles, sign up for a range of free newsletters and receive exclusive discounts and offers on Packt books and eBooks.

https://www.packtpub.com/mapt

Get the most in-demand software skills with Mapt. Mapt gives you full access to all Packt books and video courses, as well as industry-leading tools to help you plan your personal development and advance your career.

Why subscribe?

- Fully searchable across every book published by Packt
- Copy and paste, print, and bookmark content
- On demand and accessible via a web browser

Customer Feedback

Thanks for purchasing this Packt book. At Packt, quality is at the heart of our editorial process. To help us improve, please leave us an honest review on this book's Amazon page at https://www.amazon.com/dp/1788299469.

If you'd like to join our team of regular reviewers, you can e-mail us at customerreviews@packtpub.com. We award our regular reviewers with free eBooks and videos in exchange for their valuable feedback. Help us be relentless in improving our products!

Table of Contents

Preface

Network automation is the use of IT controls to supervise and carry out everyday network management functions. It plays a key role in network virtualization technologies and network functions.

This book starts by providing an introduction to network automation, SDN, and various applications of network automation, which include integrating DevOps tools to automate the network efficiently. It then guides you through different network automation tasks and covers various data digging and reporting methodologies, such as IPv6 migration, DC relocations, and interface parsing, all the while retaining security and improving data center robustness. The book then moves on to the use of Python and the management of SSH keys for machine-to-machine (M2M) communication, all followed by practical use cases. It also covers the importance of Ansible for network automation, including best practices in automation, ways to test automated networks using different tools, and other important techniques.

By the end of the book, you will be well acquainted with the various aspects of network automation.

What this book covers

Chapter 1, *Fundamental Concepts*, introduces how to get started with automation.

Chapter 2, *Python for Network Engineers*, introduces to Python as a scripting language, and samples to explain usage of Python in accessing network devices and data parsing from the device outputs.

Chapter 3, *Accessing and Mining Data from Network*, introduces you to delivering on-demand, self-service capacity and resources while retaining security and improving data center robustness.

Chapter 4, *Web Framework for Automation Triggers*, discusses making scalable calls to automation framework and generating custom and dynamic HTML pages.

Chapter 5, *Ansible for Network Automation*, explains how to virtualize Oracle databases and scale dynamically to ensure service level are met.

Chapter 6, *Continuous Integration for Network Engineers*, gives an overview of integration principles for network engineers to manage rapid growth with high availability and rapid disaster recovery.

Chapter 7, *SDN Concepts in Network Automation*, talks about moving your enterprise Java applications to virtualized x86 platforms to better utilize resources with easier life cycle and scalability management.

What you need for this book

The hardware and software requirements for this book are Python (3.5 onward), IIS, Windows, Linux, an Ansible installation, and GNS3 (for testing) or real routers.

You need an internet connection for downloading the Python libraries. Also, basic knowledge of Python, knowledge of networking, and basic familiarity with web servers like IIS are required.

Who this book is for

If you are a network engineer looking for an extensive guide to help you automate and manage your network efficiently, then this book is for you.

Conventions

In this book, you will find a number of text styles that distinguish between different kinds of information. Here are some examples of these styles and an explanation of their meaning. Code words in text, database table names, folder names, filenames, file extensions, pathnames, dummy URLs, user input, and Twitter handles are shown as follows: "From the installation directory, we just need to invoke `python.exe`, which will invoke the Python interpreter."

A block of code is set as follows:

```
#PowerShell sample code
$myvalue=$args[0]
write-host ("Argument passed to Powershell is "+$myvalue)
```

Any command-line input or output is written as follows:

```
python checkargs.py 5 6
```

New terms and **important words** are shown in bold.

> Warnings or important notes appear like this.

> Tips and tricks appear like this.

Reader feedback

Feedback from our readers is always welcome. Let us know what you think about this book-what you liked or disliked. Reader feedback is important for us as it helps us develop titles that you will really get the most out of. To send us general feedback, simply email `feedback@packtpub.com`, and mention the book's title in the subject of your message. If there is a topic that you have expertise in and you are interested in either writing or contributing to a book, see our author guide at `www.packtpub.com/authors`.

Customer support

Now that you are the proud owner of a Packt book, we have a number of things to help you to get the most from your purchase.

Downloading the example code

You can download the example code files for this book from your account at `http://www.packtpub.com`. If you purchased this book elsewhere, you can visit `http://www.packtpub.com/support` and register to have the files emailed directly to you. You can download the code files by following these steps:

1. Log in or register to our website using your email address and password.
2. Hover the mouse pointer on the **SUPPORT** tab at the top.
3. Click on **Code Downloads & Errata**.
4. Enter the name of the book in the **Search** box.

5. Select the book for which you're looking to download the code files.
6. Choose from the drop-down menu where you purchased this book from.
7. Click on **Code Download**.

Once the file is downloaded, please make sure that you unzip or extract the folder using the latest version of:

- WinRAR / 7-Zip for Windows
- Zipeg / iZip / UnRarX for Mac
- 7-Zip / PeaZip for Linux

The code bundle for the book is also hosted on GitHub at `https://github.com/PacktPublishing/Practical-Network-Automation`. We also have other code bundles from our rich catalog of books and videos available at `https://github.com/PacktPublishing/`. Check them out!

Downloading the color images of this book

We also provide you with a PDF file that has color images of the screenshots/diagrams used in this book. The color images will help you better understand the changes in the output. You can download this file from `https://www.packtpub.com/sites/default/files/downloads/PracticalNetworkAutomation_ColorImages.pdf`.

Errata

Although we have taken every care to ensure the accuracy of our content, mistakes do happen. If you find a mistake in one of our books-maybe a mistake in the text or the code-we would be grateful if you could report this to us. By doing so, you can save other readers from frustration and help us improve subsequent versions of this book. If you find any errata, please report them by visiting `http://www.packtpub.com/submit-errata`, selecting your book, clicking on the **Errata Submission Form** link, and entering the details of your errata. Once your errata are verified, your submission will be accepted and the errata will be uploaded to our website or added to any list of existing errata under the Errata section of that title. To view the previously submitted errata, go to `https://www.packtpub.com/books/content/support` and enter the name of the book in the search field. The required information will appear under the **Errata** section.

Piracy

Piracy of copyrighted material on the internet is an ongoing problem across all media. At Packt, we take the protection of our copyright and licenses very seriously. If you come across any illegal copies of our works in any form on the internet, please provide us with the location address or website name immediately so that we can pursue a remedy. Please contact us at copyright@packtpub.com with a link to the suspected pirated material. We appreciate your help in protecting our authors and our ability to bring you valuable content.

Questions

If you have a problem with any aspect of this book, you can contact us at questions@packtpub.com, and we will do our best to address the problem.

1
Fundamental Concepts

This chapter introduces the concept of network automation and familiarizes you with the keywords that are part of the automation framework. Before we dive into the details of network automation, it is important to understand why we need network automation and what we can achieve if we embrace the automation concepts and framework. This chapter also provides an insight into the traditional model of engineer and support operations, and shows how network automation can help bridge that gap for better efficiency and reliability.

Some of the topics covered in this chapter are as follows:

- What is network automation?
- DevOps
- Software-defined networking
- Basics of OpenFlow
- Basic programming concepts
- Programming language choices for automation
- Introduction to REST framework

Network automation

Automation, as the word suggests, is a framework of automating a particular task by understanding, interpreting, and creating logic. This includes enhancing the current capabilities of the tasks that are done manually and reducing the error rate of those tasks while focusing on scaling the task with reduced effort.

As an example, imagine we need to upgrade the IOS image of a Cisco router. This can involve multiple tasks, such as loading the image on the router, validating the checksum of the image, offloading traffic (if it's a production router), modifying the boot variable, and finally, reloading the router with the new image.

All of this is feasible if we have only one router to upgrade. Now take a similar scenario and try to implement it for around 1,000 routers.

Let's say we take 30 minutes getting each router to perform the aforementioned tasks. It's an easy calculation of 1000*30=30,000 minutes of manual effort.

Also, if we are performing tasks on each router manually, think of the errors that can creep in.

Network automation would be helpful in this scenario, as it can take care of all the preceding aspects and perform the tasks in parallel. Hence, if it takes 30 minutes of manual effort for one router, and in the worst case scenario the same 30 minutes for automation to perform the same task, then parallel execution would result in all 1,000 routers being upgraded within the same 30 minutes.

Hence, final amount of time will be only 30 minutes, irrespective of the number of routers you throw at the automation framework. This also drastically reduces the need for manual work, and an engineer can focus on any failures in the 1,000 network devices.

In the upcoming sections, I will introduce you to some of the concepts, tools, and examples that will get you started with building automation frameworks and effectively using them in network scenarios to perform network-related activities.

This also assumes that you have an idea of network concepts and common terminology used in networking.

Some of the examples that I will provide assume familiarity with syslog, TACACS, basic router configs such as hostnames, iOS image loading, basic routing and switching concepts, and **Simple Network Management Protocol (SNMP)**.

DevOps

Historically, there have been two specific teams in every networking department. One of the teams is the engineering team, which is responsible for conceiving new ideas to improve the network and designing, deploying, and optimizing the current infrastructure. This team is primarily responsible for performing tasks such as configuration and cabling from scratch.

The other team is the support team. This team, also known as the operations team, ensures the current deployed infrastructure is up and running and focuses on performing day-to-day activities such as upgrades, quick fixes, and support to any consumers of that network infrastructure. In a traditional model, there are hand-offs and knowledge transfers from the engineering team to the operations team for support of the current deployed infrastructure. Because of the segregation of the two teams, the engineer team members do not focus on writing clear documentation, or sometimes do not even provide adequate information to operations team members, causing delays in troubleshooting and fixing issues. This could even lead to a simple solution scaling to a bigger problem because of the different approach that a engineering team member would take compared to an operations team member.

Nowadays, to solve this problem, the DevOps model was conceived, which brings the best from both teams. Rather than being a fancy designation, a DevOps model is a culture that needs to be created among the current teams. In a DevOps model, an engineer from any team is responsible for the complete life cycle of a specific project. This includes creating part of the infrastructure and supporting it by themselves. A big benefit of this model is that because a person has created a part of the system and supports it, they know all the aspects of that part and can work on it again to make it better by understanding the challenges that arise from customer or user experiences. A DevOps engineer should understand the engineering and operations for the part of the infrastructure that they have created. By adding an automation skill set to the DevOps experience, an engineer can manage complex tasks with ease and focus on reliability and scalability in a better manner than engineers who are distributed in different domains in the traditional model.

Software-defined networking

As you may be aware, there have been multiple proprietary networking devices, such as firewalls, switches, and routers, that were made by different network vendors. However, owing to the proprietary information from each different vendor, multiple network devices might not exist in a single network infrastructure environment. Even if they exist together, network engineers have to focus their effort on ensuring that each vendor device can exist in a network path without any hiccups. There might be times when one routing protocol might not be compatible with all the network devices in a multi-vendor environment, and a lot of time is wasted ensuring either the removal of that protocol, or the removal of the vendor which that does not support that protocol. This can waste effort and time, which could be better spent improving the infrastructure.

To solve this type of issue, **software-defined networking (SDN)** has been introduced. In an SDN scenario, a packet flow is defined from a central controller that in turn interacts with multi-vendor equipment to create/define rules based upon the required packet flow. This shifts the focus of a network engineer entirely to how the traffic flows, which path the packet takes, to even responding to link down situations through automated routing of packets by configuring some rules or policies on the controllers. Another advantage of SDN is that the multi-vendor equipment is now not the center piece of infrastructure. The focus shifts to how optimally the routing and traffic shaping (the process to identify the optimal path of traffic flow) is occurring. As part of Software driven tasks, there are pieces of code that are specifically written to control a specific task or goal (similar to functions or methods in programming). This piece of code is triggered by controller decisions or rules, which in turn adds, modifies, or deletes configs on the multi-vendor device to ensure the rule set on the controller is adhered to. SDN even has the ability to completely isolate a failure domain, through the identification of a physical link down or even a total device failure without affecting the flow of traffic in real time. For example, a switch can issue a request to the controller if it gets a packet destined for a network that it does not know. This would be a packet drop or route not found in a traditional network model, but with SDN, it is the task of a controller to provide the destination or path information to the switches to correctly route the packet.

This ensures the troubleshooting becomes much easier, since a network engineer now has full control of each path/packet flow, irrespective of the vendor-specific protocol or technology support. Additionally, since now we are following a standard set of protocols, we can even lower our costs by removing more expensive proprietary network devices and replacing them with open standards network gear.

OpenFlow

OpenFlow is a communication protocol that is used for communication between different vendor's equipment for the packet flow. This standard is maintained by a group called **Open Network Foundation (ONF)**. OpenFlow, as the name suggests, is used to control the flow of packets in a network layer through a mix of **Access Control Lists (ACLs)** and routing protocols.

OpenFlow primarily has two components—controllers and switches. Controllers are used to take decisions in terms of creating a path for the packet to flow across the different connected devices, and switches (or network equipment) are dynamically configured from the controller based upon the path that a packet needs to take.

Going a little more in-depth, OpenFlow controllers control the routing of packets in OpenFlow switch forwarding tables through the modification, addition, or deletion of packet matching rules as decided by the controller.

As OpenFlow is another protocol, it runs over TCP and works on port 6653 on controllers. At the time of writing, OpenFlow standard 1.4 is currently active and being widely used in the SDN framework. OpenFlow is an additional service that proprietary network vendors run alongside their custom software. This, in general, ensures that the data forwarding or data packet handling is still part of proprietary switch, but the data flow or control plane tasks is now taken over by OpenFlow controllers. As part of SDN framework, if a participating switch receives a packet and does not know where to send it, it communicates with the OpenFlow controller for an answer. The controller, based upon its preconfigured logic, decides what action to take for that unknown packet and can get switches that it is controlling to create a separate or a specific path for that packet to flow across the network. Because of this behavior, this is the protocol that is currently being deployed across all deployments where SDN is being introduced.

Program concepts

Now, as we start working upon our practical approach to automation, we need to understand the basics of what a program is and how to write one.

Simply explained, a program is a set of instructions that is passed to the system to perform a specific task. This set of instructions is based upon real-life challenges and tasks that need to be accomplished in an automated method. Small sets of programs can be combined to create an application that can be installed, deployed, and configured for individual or organizational requirements. Some of the key concepts and programming techniques that we will discuss from this point onward will be PowerShell and Python. These are the two most popular scripting languages that are used to create quick, effective, and result-oriented automation.

These are some of the key concepts that I would like to introduce while creating a program:

- Variables
- Data types
- Decision makers
- Loops
- Arrays
- Functions
- Best practices

Variables

These are predefined, human-readable, and understandable words or letters that are used to store some values. At the very basis of writing a program we need a variable in which we will store the data or information, and based upon the variables, we can further enhance the programming logic. As we can see in the first line, an important part of creating a variable is that it should be human-readable and understandable.

Let us take an example: Suppose I want to store a number 2 in a variable. We can choose any name for a variable and define it:

```
Option 1: x=2
Option 2: number=2
```

The correct answer will be Option 2, as we know by the variable name (number) that this variable contains a specific number. As we can see in the preceding example, if we keep on using random ways of defining variables as we would when creating a big program, the complexity would be increased substantially because of the unclear meanings of the variables.

Different programming languages have different ways to define a variable, but the underlying concept of ensuring a variable is human-readable should be the top-most priority of the programmer or program author.

Data types

As the name suggests, these are the classifications of the values that we pass on to the variable. A variable can be defined to store a specific type of value that can be declared based upon the data type.

There are multiple data types, but for our initial discussion there are primarily four data types that need to be understood:

- **String**: This is a catch-all data type. Any value defined as a string is as simple as saying the value is plain English with characters, alphabets, special characters, and so on. I have referred to it as a catch-all data type because nearly all other data types can be converted to string format keeping the same values intact during conversion to string.

Consider the following example:

```
number=2
```

This defines that a variable named `number` has a value of 2.
Similarly, if we declare:

```
string_value="2"
```

This is same as saying that a value of 2 has been now defined as string and stored in a variable named `string_value`.

- **Integer**: This specifies that any value that is a number needs to be defined with this data type. The key thing to note here is that an integer value will contain a whole number and not a decimal value:

Consider an example as follows:

```
integernumber=2
```

This defines that a variable named as `integernumber` has a value of the number 2.
An incorrect assignation here would be something like:

```
integernumber=2.4
```

This would give an error in some programming languages as an integer needs to be interpreted as a whole number and not a decimal value.

- **Float**: This data type removes the restriction that we saw earlier with integer. It simply means we can have a decimal number and can perform mathematical calculations and storage of decimal values in a float data type.
- **Datetime**: This is an extended data type found in a lot of modern scripting languages. This data type ensures that the values that are being stored or retrieved are in date format. This is typically useful if we need to create a program that uses some time or date calculations. As an example, perhaps we need to find out how many syslogs were generated from a router in the last seven days. The last seven days will be stored by this data type.

Decision makers

These are one of the very critical components of a program and they can define the flow of the program. As the name suggests, a decision maker decides a certain action based upon a certain condition.

Simply put, if you wanted to buy an ice cream you would go to an ice-cream shop, but for a coffee you would go to a coffee shop. In this case, the condition was whether you wanted ice cream or coffee. The action was based upon the result of the condition: you went to that specific shop.

These decision makers, also called **conditions**, are defined in a different manner in different scripting languages, but the result of each of the conditions decides the future flow of the program.

Generally, in a condition, two or more values are compared and either a true or a false is returned. Depending on the value returned, a specific set of instructions are executed.

Consider the following example:

```
Condition:
if (2 is greater than 3), then
Proceed to perform Option 1
else
Proceed to perform Option 2
```

As we see in the preceding example, a condition is evaluated and if 2 is greater than 3, then the flow of program will be performed based upon Option 1, and in case of a false (which means 2 is not greater than 3), Option 2 would be chosen.

If we want a bit more complexity, we can add multiple decision-making statements or conditions to granulize the flow of a program.

Let us take an example:

```
if (Car is of red color), then
  if (Car is Automatic), then
    if (Car is a sedan), then
      Option 1 (Purchase the car)
    else (Option 2, ask for a sedan car from dealer)
  else (Option 3, ask for an Automatic car from dealer)
else (Option 4, ask for a red car from dealer)
```

As we can see in this complex condition, we can easily decide the flow of a program based upon additional checks. In this case, I only want to buy a `Car` that is `red`, `Automatic`, and a `sedan`. If any of those conditions are not met, then I ask the dealer to meet that specific condition.

Another thing to notice in the preceding example is that the conditions are nested within each other, hence they are shown as nested with spaces deciding the sub-conditions from its parent condition. This is usually depicted within brackets or with simple indentation based upon the scripting language used.

Sometimes, it is necessary to evaluate a value against multiple conditions and perform an action if it matches any of the conditions. This is called a **switch case** in programming.

Consider an example as follows:

```
Carcolor="Red" (Here we define a variable if the value of string as Red)
switch (Carcolor)
Case (Red) (Perform Option 1)
Case (Blue) (Perform Option 2)
Case (Green) (Perform Option 3)
```

Here we see that depending upon the variable's value, a certain type of action can be performed. In this case, option 1 will be performed. If we change the value of the `Carcolor` variable to `Blue`, then option 2 will be performed.

An important component of conditions are the comparison operators that we use to compare two values for the result. Some example operators are equal to, greater than, less than, and not equal to. Depending on which comparison operator we use, the results can vary.

Let us take an example:

```
greaternumber=5
lessernumber=6

if (greaternumber 'greater than' lessernumber)
Perform Option 1
else
Perform Option 2
```

We declare two variables named `greaternumber` and `lessernumber` and compare them in a condition. The conditional operator we use is `greater than`, which would result in option 1 if the condition is true (`greaternumber` is greater than `lessernumber`), or would result in option 2 if the condition is false (`greaternumber` is not greater than `lessernumber`).

Additionally, we also have operators that are called logical operators, such as AND, OR, or NOT. We can combine more than one condition by using these logical operators. They have a similar meaning in English, which means that if, for example, we use the AND operator, we want condition 1 AND condition 2 both to be true before we perform an action.

Consider an example: I want to buy a car only when the `car is red`, `automatic`, and a `sedan`:

```
if (car is 'red') AND (car is 'automatic') AND (car is 'sedan')
Perform action 'buy car'
else
Perform action 'do not buy'
```

This simply means I would evaluate all the three conditions and only if all of them are true, then I would perform the action `buy car`. In this case, if any of the conditions do not meet the values, such as the car is blue, then the `do not buy` action will be performed.

Loops

A loop, as we know in common language, is circling the same path over and over again. In other words, if I am asked to fetch five ice creams from the ice cream store, and I can carry only one ice cream at a time, I will repeat the process of going to the ice cream shop to purchase ice cream five times. Correlating this with programming, if the same set of instructions need to be performed multiple times, then we put those instructions inside a loop.

A very basic loop is generally depicted as an iteration of a variable as many times as we want the instructions to be carried out.

Let's take an example:

```
Start the loop from one, until the loop has been repeated sixty times,
adding a value of 1 to the loop:
Perform action
```

If you see the instructions being passed, there are three separate segments that are depicted in a loop:

1. `Start the loop from one`: This means that the loop should start with a value of one.
2. `until the loop has been repeated sixty times`: This means perform the same set of tasks until the loop has completed sixty turns of execution.
3. `adding a value of 1 to the loop`: This means that we dictate that after completion of each round of loop, increment the loop count by 1.

The result will be the same action performed sixty times, until the loop count reaches sixty. Additionally, a loop can used to iterate through multiple values stored in a variable irrespective of whether it is an integer, string, or any other data type.

Arrays

An array (or list in some scripting languages) is used to store a similar set of multiple values inside a single variable. This helps to ensure all data types with similar meanings are stored in a single variable, and also we can easily loop through these array objects to fetch the values stored in an array.

Consider the following example:

```
countries=["India","China","USA","UK"]
for specific country in countries
 Perform action
```

As we can see in the variable declaration, now we are declaring a similar data type with a similar context or meaning by grouping them together and assigning them into a single variable. In our example, it's the country names all assigned to an array variable named `countries`. In the next line, we are now iterating using the loop method, and for every `specific country` in the list or array of `countries`, we will perform the action. In this case, the loop will be executed to perform the action for each country, from the country name `India` to the end of the country name `UK`.

Each value stored in an array is referred to as an element of the array. Additionally, an array can be easily sorted, which means irrespective of the order of the elements in the array, we can get a sorted list or array by calling some additional programming tasks.

Let's consider an example:

```
countries=["India",  "China",  "USA","UK"]
Sort (countries)
```

The result will be as follows:

```
countries=["China","India","UK",USA"]
```

The sort functionality ensured that all the elements inside the array are sorted alphabetically and stored in the sorted order.

Functions

Functions or methods are a pre-written small set of instructions that result in a specific task being performed when they are called. The functions can also be defined as a single name for a group of programming instructions written together to achieve a common task.

Taking an example, think of driving as a function. In driving, there are multiple things that need to be taken care of, such as understanding traffic signals, running a car, and driving the car in traffic and on the road.

All these tasks are grouped in a function named `driving`. Now, let's say we have two people, example 1 and example 2, who want to learn to drive. From a programming perspective, once we define a function, we need to call it whenever we want to perform the same set of tasks. Hence, we would call `driving(example 1)` and then `driving (example 2)`, which would ensure that both people would become a driver after going through the set of instructions in the `driving` function.

Let us look at another example:

```
countries=["India","China","USA","UK"]

function hellocountry(countryname)
 Return "hello " countryname

for each country in countries:
     hellocountry(each country)
```

In the first line, we declare an array with country names as elements. Next, we define a function named `hellocountry` that accepts an input of `countryname`. In the function itself, we simply return the value of the `countryname` that was passed to the function as input, preceding by the work `hello`.

Now all that remains is to iterate through all the elements of countries and pass each `countryname` as input to the `hellocountry` function. As we can see, we called the same function for each element, and based upon the instructions declared inside the function, that specific task was now performed for each element in the array.

Best practices

As we have now looked at the basics of some of the key components of a program, there is another important aspect of how to write a good program that we will consider.

From a machine's perspective, there is no understanding of how a program is written, as long as the instructions given in the program are in the right format or syntax and the machine is able to interpret each of the instructions correctly. For an end user, again the way the program is written might not be important as long as the end user gets the desired result. The person concerned with how a program is written is a programmer who is writing their own program, or a programmer or developer who needs to interpret another programmer's program.

There may be multiple reasons why a programmer might need to interpret a program that's not been written by them. It may be to support the program while the programmer who wrote the program is not available, or to enhance the program by adding their own piece of code or programming instructions. Another reason for code readability is fixing bugs. Any program or set of instructions may malfunction due to incorrect input or incorrect logic, which can result in unexpected behavior or unexpected results. This is called a bug, and bugs need to be fixed to ensure the program does what it was written for originally.

Every programmer has their own set of best practices, but some of the key aspects of a program are readability, support information, and indentation.

Readability of a program

This is one of the most important aspects of writing a good program. A program needs to be written in such a way that even a layman or a first-time reader of the program should be able to interpret the basics of what is happening.

Variables need to be declared properly so that each variable makes it clear what it stores:

```
x="India"
y="France"
```

could have been written better like this:

```
asiancountry="India"
europecountry="France"
```

Here's another example:

```
x=5
y=2
```

It could be written like this:

```
biggernumber=5
smallernumber=2
```

As we can see in the preceding example, if we write a two- or three-line program, we can easily declare the variables in a random way, but things become much more complex, even for a programmer writing their own program, when these random variables are used in a longer program. Just imagine if you have declared the variables as a, b, c, and so on, and later, after using even 10 or 15 more variables, you need to go back to each line of the program to understand what value was declared in a, b, or c.

Another aspect of writing a good program is commenting. Different scripting languages provide different ways of commenting a program. Comments are necessary to ensure we break the flow of each program into sections, with each section having a comment explaining the use of that section. A very good example is if you declare a function. A function named Cooking, for example, and another function named CookingPractice might sound confusing because of their names. Now, if we add a comment to the Cooking method saying *this function is to master the art of cooking when you have learned how to cook*, and add a comment to CookingPractice saying *this method is to learn cooking*, this can make things very easy for someone reading through the program.

A programmer now can easily interpret that whenever he wants to learn to cook, he has to call CookingPractice and not the Cooking method. Comments don't have any special meaning in any programming language, and they are ignored when the machine is trying to convert the programming language to machine instructions. Hence, comments are only for programmers and to make readers aware of what is happening in a program. A comment should also be placed with every complex condition, loop, and so on, to clarify the usage of that specific condition or loop.

Support information

This, as the name suggests, is additional information, preferably added as comments, containing details about the program and author. As a suggestion, at the minimum a program should have the author info (that is, the person who created the program), contact details such as phone number and email address, basic usage of the program or the purpose of the program, and the version of the program.

The version is specific such as starting from 1.0 and as and when we enhance the program or add new features, we can change it to version 1.1 (for minor changes) or a newer version such as version 2.0 (for major changes).

Consider an example:

```
Program start
Comment: Author: Myself
Comment: Contact: myemail@emailaddress.com
Comment: Phone: 12345
Comment: Version: 1.0
Comment: Purpose: This program is to demo the comments for support info
Comment: Execution method: Open the Command Prompt and run this program by
calling this program.
Comment: Any extra additional info (if needed)

Program end
```

This approach ensures that everyone knows which is the latest version of the script and how to execute the program or script. Also, this has info about the contact details of the author, so if anything breaks in production, the author can be easily reached to rectify or fix the scripts in production.

Indentation

This is similar to what we do when we write in plain English. Indenting a program is mandatory in some scripting languages, but as a best practice it should be followed for any program that we write in any programming language. Indentation improves the readability of a program because it helps the programmer or someone else reading the program to quickly understand the flow of the program.

Let's see an example where we have a nested condition in which we check if a Car is Red and if it is a Sedan and if it is Automatic.
A bad way of writing this would be as follows:

```
if (Car is 'Red')
if (Car is 'Sedan')
if (Car is 'Automatic')
do something
```

Now, think of adding multiple lines like this to a long program, and you will get easily confused by the flow of program as you read through it.
A better and recommended way to write this is as follows:

```
if (Car is 'Red')
    if (Car is 'Sedan')
        if (Car is 'Automatic')
            do something
```

This provides a clear flow of the program. Only check the other conditions if the Car is Red; otherwise, don't check for the other conditions. This is where we say we are nesting the conditions inside each other, which is also called **nested conditions**.

This also clears a lot of confusion while troubleshooting a complex program. We can easily identify the problematic code or instructions by quickly parsing through the program and understanding the flow for each segment of the program.

Sample best practice example

This example summarizes the best practices using all the elements that we have learned so far, by creating a basic program.

Problem statement: Parse all the countries declared in an array and only print the names of those countries that contain the letter I or letter U in their names:

```
Program begin:

Comment: This is a sample program to explain best practice
Comment: Author name: Programmer
Comment: Email: Programmer@programming.com
Version: 1.0

Comment: The following section declares the list of countries in array
countrylist
countrylist=['India','US','UK','France','China','Japan']
```

```
function validatecountryname(countryname)
    Comment: This function takes the input of countryname, checks if it
contains I or U and returns value based upon the result.
    if ((countryname contains 'I') OR (countryname contains 'U')
        return "Countryname contains I or U"
    else
        return "Countryname does not contain I our U"

Comment: This is a loop that parses each countryname from the countrylist
one by one and sends the variable 'countryname' as input to function
validatecoutryname

foreach countryname in countrylist
    validatecountryname (countryname)

Comment: Program ends here
```

The program is self-explanatory, but it is worth noting the support comments such as author, email, and so on. The indentation ensures that any reader has a clear idea of the flow of program.

Additionally, another thing to observe is the use of names that clearly depict the usage of the variable or name. Each variable and function name clearly specifies what it is being used for. The additional comment lines in between add clarity on what each segment is doing and the purpose of the statement or function.

Language choices (Python/PowerShell)

Moving ahead, armed with the knowledge of how to write a program and an understanding best practices, we will now look at some scripting languages that suffice for our automation scripts. A basic difference between a scripting language and a programming language (such as C and C++) is that a scripting language is not compiled but interpreted through the underlying environment in which it is executed (in other words, a converter is required to convert the commands written in human-readable format to machine format by parsing one line at a time), whereas the programming language is primarily compiled and hence can be executed in multiple environments without the use of any specific underlying environment or requirements.

What this means is if I write a script in Python, PowerShell, or even Perl, I need to install that specific language in order to run the program or script that I have written. C or C++ code can be compiled to make an executable file (.exe), and can run independently without the installation of any language. Additionally, a scripting language is less code-intensive, which means that it can automatically interpret some of the code written in a program depending on how it is called.

Let's consider an example. Here's how we declare a variable in scripting language:

```
x=5
```

OR

```
x="author"
```

OR

```
x=3.5
```

Whereas in a programming language, the same type of declaration would be made like this:

```
integer x=5
String x="author"
Float x=3.5
```

This states that depending on the value we assign to the variable, the variable type is automatically identified in an scripting language, whereas in a programming language the declarations are tightly controlled. In this case, if we declare a variable as a String, this clearly means that we cannot declare any other type of value in that variable unless we explicitly change the data type of that variable.

We have primarily three types of scripting language that are popular for creating programs and are mainly used for automation scripting or programming. These are Perl, Python, and PowerShell.

With support for the oldest language, Perl, diminishing, the focus is now on Python because of its open source support and on PowerShell because of its Microsoft, or .NET environment. Comparing both languages is not ideal because it's up to the reader which programming language they use to write their programs. As we have more than 70% of computers running Windows, and with a growing market of Microsoft Azure as a cloud operating system from Microsoft, PowerShell is the preferred language owing to the underlying .NET environment. As we create a program in PowerShell, it is easy to port that program and execute it on another machine running Windows without any special settings.

Python, on the other hand, is growing in popularity because of its open source approach. There are thousands of developers who contribute to enhancing Python by adding special functions for specific tasks. For example, there is a function or sub-program, called `Paramiko`, that is used to log into network routers. Another one is `Netmiko`, which is an enhanced version of `Paramiko` that is used to log into network devices based upon network hardware vendor and operating systems (such as Cisco iOS or Cisco NXOS). Python needs to be installed before writing a Python program and successfully executing it.

Going forward, our focus will be on Python, with additional tips and tricks on how to perform the same tasks using PowerShell instead of Python.

Writing your first program

Now, because we are starting from fresh, we need to understand how to write our first program and execute it. PowerShell comes pre-installed on a Windows machine. But we need to install Python by downloading it from the web (`https://www.python.org`) and choosing the right version for your operating system. Once downloaded, it can installed just like any other application that is installed on a Windows machine.

On a Linux machine, the same holds true, but because of the .NET requirement, PowerShell will not be supported on Linux or Unix environments. Hence, if we are using a Unix or Linux environment, Python or Perl remain our preferences for scripting.

There are multiple **Integrated Development Environments (IDEs)** for both Python and PowerShell, but the default ones that come with these languages are also pretty helpful.

There are multiple versions of PowerShell and Python being used. When writing programs in higher versions, generally the backwards support is not very good, so make sure you note the users and environment before choosing a version.

In our case, we will be using PowerShell 4 and Python 3 onwards for writing programs. Some commands might not run in older versions of PowerShell and Python, and some syntax or commands are different in older versions.

PowerShell IDE

This can be invoked by clicking on the **Start** button and searching for **Windows PowerShell ISE**. Once invoked, the initial screen will look like this:

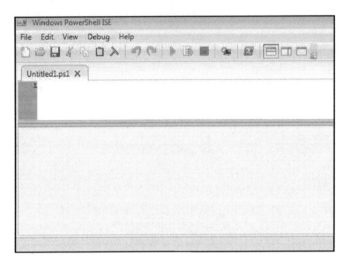

As we can see in the preceding screenshot, a PowerShell script is saved with a .ps1 extension. Once we write something in the IDE (or ISE, as it is called with PowerShell), it needs to be saved as somefilename.ps1 and then executed to see the result.

Let's take write a program called Hello World:

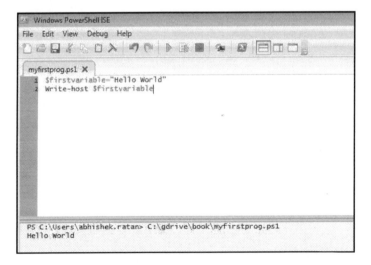

- As we can see in our first program, we write two lines to print Hello World. In the ISE, we pass the commands to declare a variable (a variable is denoted by a dollar sign, $, in front of the variable in PowerShell), assigning the value Hello World to it. The next line is simply printing that variable by calling a method or function called Write-host, which is used to print values onscreen in PowerShell.
- Once we write the program and save it, the next step is execution to see our result.
- The green button at the top of the ISE is used to execute the script, and the result of the script is shown at the bottom of the screen. In this case, it was a simple Hello World output.

PowerShell scripts can also be invoked directly by the command line. As PowerShell is a scripting language and needs to be installed on a machine, we can directly call PowerShell from the Windows Command Prompt and execute the scripts and individual scripting commands from the PowerShell console itself.

This is how we can find out the version of PowerShell:

As we can see in the preceding screenshot, PowerShell is invoked by calling powershell directly from the Command Prompt in Windows. When PowerShell is invoked, we see PS before the command line, which confirms that we are now inside the PowerShell console. To see the version, we call a system variable, $psversiontable, which shows the version of PowerShell.

We can see that this is version 2.x (as shown in CLRVersion). System variables are special variables that have predefined values based upon the installation types. These special variables can be called at any time in our script to fetch their values and perform actions based upon the returned values.

The following example shows that we are using a higher version of PowerShell:

```
C:\>powershell
Windows PowerShell
Copyright (C) 2014 Microsoft Corporation. All rights reserved.

PS C:\> $psversiontable

Name                            Value
----                            -----
PSVersion                       4.0
WSManStackVersion               3.0
SerializationVersion            1.1.0.1
CLRVersion                      4.0.30319.42000
BuildVersion                    6.3.9600.18728
PSCompatibleVersions            {1.0, 2.0, 3.0, 4.0}
PSRemotingProtocolVersion       2.2


PS C:\>
```

As we can see, the same variable now returns a value of 4.0 for PSVersion, which confirms that this is version 4 of PowerShell.

 PowerShell 4.0 is the default installation from Windows 8.1 onwards on client operating system, and Windows Server 2012 R2 in a Server environment.

Python IDE

Similar to PowerShell, once Python is installed, it has its own IDE. It can be invoked by typing or calling IDLE (Python) from the **Start** menu:

```
Python 3.6.1 Shell
File  Edit  Shell  Debug  Options  Window  Help
Python 3.6.1 (v3.6.1:69c0db5, Mar 21 2017, 17:54:52) [MSC v.1900 32 bit (Intel)]
on win32
Type "copyright", "credits" or "license()" for more information.
>>> |
```

The Python IDE, called IDLE, looks similar to the preceding screenshot when it is opened. The heading bar depicts the version of Python (which is 3.6.1 in this case) and the three greater than signs (>>>) show the command line, which is ready to accept Python commands and execute them. To write a program, we click on **File | New File**, which opens up a notepad in which we can write the program.

Lets see a similar `hello world` program in Python:

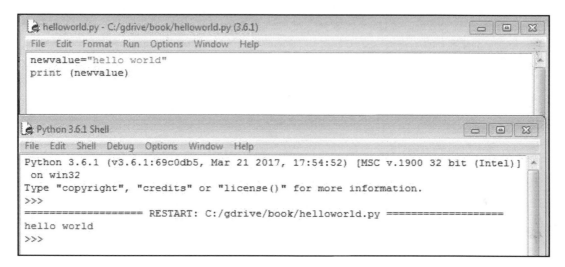

As we write a new program, the variable used is `newvalue`, and the value assigned to it is `hello world`. The next line is simply calling Python's `print` function to print the value inside the variable during the execution of the script.

Once we have written the program, we click on **File | Save As** in the window where we wrote the program, and save the script. The script is saved as `filename.py`, with the `.py` extension denoting a Python script. Once it is saved, we can press the *F5* button on the keyboard or select **Run | Run Module** in the script window to run that specific script. The following window is the same window that was invoked when we first called the IDLE application from the **Start** menu, but now it has the output of that script that we wrote.

The output of `hello world` is now seen in the IDLE window. Once we are done with writing the script or Python commands, we can simply close the open command windows to close the application or Python interpreter.

Similar to PowerShell, we can also call `python` from the command line, as follows:

One additional thing to notice here is that to exit the Python interpreter, we call the `exit()` function. This tells Python to stop the execution and exit to the Command Prompt in Windows.

Representational State Transfer (REST) framework

One of the most important aspects of network automation is to understand and leverage tools that are currently available for specific tasks. For example, this could be Splunk for data mining, SolarWinds for network monitoring, syslog servers, or even any custom applications to perform various tasks.

Another important aspect of writing an application is how we can utilize the same application for additional tasks without altering the application itself. In other words, let's say we buy a car for our personal use, but an enhancement of this would be using the same car as a taxi or in some other role.

This is we introduce the **Application Program Interface (API)**. APIs are used to expose some aspect of an already written application to merge with the programs that we are writing so that we can easily call that specific task using a specific API. For example, as SolarWinds is a specialized application that is used for network monitoring and other purposes, we can call the API of SolarWinds to get the network device list in our script. Hence, we leave the specialized task of discovering the network devices on the network to SolarWinds, but we utilize its expertise in our script through the API of that application.

Getting a bit deeper, the API is nothing more than a function (similar to the functions that we write in our scripts); the only difference is what values those functions return. An API function generally returns the values in **Extended Markup Language (XML)** or **JavaScript Object Notation (JSON)** format, which are industry standards of cross-environment and cross-machine information exchange. Think of this as similar to how we communicate with each other using English as a common language. Although we may have been born in different cultures, in different countries, we can use English to communicate with each other effectively, since English is the industry standard of human interaction. Similarly, irrespective of how a program is written, in whatever language (such as C, C++, Java, VB, C#, and so on), each program can talk to another program by calling its APIs and the results come in either XML or JSON.

XML is a standard way of encoding results and sending them across to the requestor and, using the same standard, the requestor can decode the results. JSON is another way in which data interactions can happen across applications.

Here is sample XML:

```
<?xml version="1.0" encoding="UTF-8"?>
<note>
  <to>Readers</to>
  <from>JAuthor</from>
  <heading>Reminder</heading>
  <body>Read this for more knowledge</body>
</note>
```

The first line in the preceding content depicts that whatever follows after that line is in XML format. The XML files are saved with extension of `.xml`.

Now as we can see, if we count the number of characters returned from an XML result, if we add the characters, such as `<heading>Reminder</heading>`, it returns results within the starting tag and ending tag of `<heading>`. This means that the size of an XML file is greatly increased owing to the overhead character counts of additional closing tags.

Here's the same example in JSON:

```
{
  "note": {
  "to": "Tove",
  "from": "Jani",
  "heading": "Reminder",
  "body": "Don't forget me this weekend!"
  }
}
```

As we can see, we have got rid of those extra bulky opening and closing tags that we saw earlier in XML. What this means is if we are calling an API to return a huge amount of data in XML format, it would certainly take a longer time to fetch that data from the application and more consumption of resources such as memory and storage to temporarily or permanently store that data. To overcome this situation, the JSON format is now preferred to XML to exchange data through APIs. JSON is lightweight and less resource-intensive than XML because of differences in the way the data is returned. JSON files are saved with the extension `.json`.

This functionality of working with APIs, back end methods, and functions written in a particular programming language to be called APIs, and functions returning values in XML or JSON format, all of which is running over web protocols such as HTTP or HTTPS, is cumulatively called the REST framework. The REST framework is the same industry standard of interacting using XML or JSON that were referenced earlier, with the addition of GET, POST, and other interactions happening over the web protocols. The HTTP requests to APIs can be GET or POST requests that the REST framework recognizes and, similar to HTTP GET and POST requests, interacts with underlying applications to perform the requested actions.

Scripting languages rely heavily on API calls, and applications that need to provide the API's functionality adhere to REST framework requirements to ensure they extend their capabilities to the scripts that are called to fetch or save data in their choice of scripting language. A big benefit of this is that cross-platform communication is now happening with neither party (the caller of API or the application providing the API's functionality) knowing which language or environment the other are running. Hence, a Windows application can easily work with a Unix environment and vice versa using this approach, with HTTP being the standard communication language for calling APIs, and parsing the results with industry standard XML or JSON formats.

The sample API REST call in PowerShell is as follows:

As we can see in the preceding screenshot, we call the `Invoke-RestMethod` function in PowerShell, which is used to call the API method of the application with the default communication and interactions using JSON.

The application called is in a REST framework, with access to the API with the URL `https:/` `/blogs.msdn.microsoft.com/powershell/feed/`. This uses the HTTPS protocol to communicate with the application.

`format-table` is a function of PowerShell that specifies that however the result comes, display the `title` property of each record/result returned from the API call. If we had not used that command, the display would have shown all the properties returned for each record.

Here's an example REST call in Python:

```
Python 3.6.1 Shell
File  Edit  Shell  Debug  Options  Window  Help
Python 3.6.1 (v3.6.1:69c0db5, Mar 21 2017, 17:54:52) [MSC v.1900 32 bit (Intel)] on win32
Type "copyright", "credits" or "license()" for more information.
>>> import requests
>>> r=requests.get('http://maps.googleapis.com/maps/api/geocode/json?address=google')
>>> r.json()
{'results': [{'address_components': [{'long_name': '111', 'short_name': '111', 'types': ['street_number']}, {
'long_name': '8th Avenue', 'short_name': '8th Ave', 'types': ['route']}, {'long_name': 'Manhattan', 'short_na
me': 'Manhattan', 'types': ['political', 'sublocality', 'sublocality_level_1']}, {'long_name': 'New York', 's
hort_name': 'New York', 'types': ['locality', 'political']}, {'long_name': 'New York County', 'short_name': '
New York County', 'types': ['administrative_area_level_2', 'political']}, {'long_name': 'New York', 'short_na
me': 'NY', 'types': ['administrative_area_level_1', 'political']}, {'long_name': 'United States', 'short_name
': 'US', 'types': ['country', 'political']}, {'long_name': '10011', 'short_name': '10011', 'types': ['postal_
code']}], 'formatted_address': '111 8th Ave, New York, NY 10011, USA', 'geometry': {'location': {'lat': 40.74
06375, 'lng': -74.0020388}, 'location_type': 'ROOFTOP', 'viewport': {'northeast': {'lat': 40.7419864802915, '
lng': -74.00069981970848}, 'southwest': {'lat': 40.7392885197085, 'lng': -74.00338778029149}}}, 'place_id': '
ChIJH_XxFL9ZwokR8F3XW7NaG8w', 'types': ['establishment', 'point_of_interest']}], 'status': 'OK'}
>>>
```

In this example, we call a standard function called `requests`. The first line, `import` `requests`, means that we are referencing the `requests` function or library to call in our Python script. On the next line, we are calling the Google Map API with JSON using a `requests.get` method. In other words, we are ensuring a HTTP GET call to the Google API URL. Once we get the result, we call the `json()` method to store the value in the variable `r`.

Sometimes, when we call a custom function or library of Python using `import`, it may give an error stating that the module has not been found. This means that it does not come with the standard Python installation and needs to be installed separately. To fix this, we can install the module manually using the `pip` or `easy_install` commands, which we will see in detail in upcoming chapters.

Summary

In this chapter, we covered the basics of various terminology that we will use while performing network automation. This chapter also introduced the readers to some basic aspects of programming to help build the logic of a program.

This chapter also explained why to write a good program and how to write one, along with some reference points for scripting languages. There was also a brief discussion about the current scripting languages, their basic usage, and writing a very basic program in two of the most popular scripting languages (Python and PowerShell).

Finally, we summed it all up by introducing the REST framework, which included a discussion about APIs, how to call them, and an explanation of XML and JSON as inter-platform data exchange languages.

The next chapter will go deeper into how to write scripts using Python, with relevant examples in PowerShell to ensure the reader becomes familiar with both Python and PowerShell. There will be tips and best practices as well.

2
Python for Network Engineers

As we are now familiar with how to write a program using the concepts used in programming languages, as well as best practices, now let's dig deep into writing an actual Python program or script. Keeping the primary focus on how to write a program in Python, we will also see how to write the same program in PowerShell, since there might be times where we would need to use PowerShell to achieve the results that we are looking for. We will cover various aspects of creating a program with some explanations of each of the statements and provide some tips and tricks to get through those tricky situations.

In this chapter, we will cover the following topics:

- Python interpreter and data types
- Writing Python scripts using conditional loops
- Functions
- Installing new modules/libraries
- Passing arguments from command line for scripts
- Using Netmiko to interact with network devices
- Multithreading

Python interpreter and data types

An interpreter, as the name suggests, is used to interpret instructions so that they are understandable by others. In our case, it is used to convert our Python language to a machine-understandable format that governs the flow of instructions that we gave to the machine.

It is also used to convert the set of values and messages given by a machine to a human-readable format in order to give us insights into how our program is being executed.

As mentioned in `Chapter 1`, *Fundamental Concepts*, the interpreter that we are focusing on is Python 3.6. I will be using it on the Windows platform, but the site has clear instructions on how to download and install the same on other OS like Unix or Linux machines. Once we install it by downloading it from the Python community which can be found at URL `https://www.python.org/downloads`, we can simply click on the setup file to install it. From the installation directory we just need to invoke `python.exe`, which will invoke the Python interpreter.

In order to call Python from anywhere in your Command Prompt, just add the Python installation folder in your PATH variable.
Here's an example: `set path=%path%;C:\python36`. This is going to add the Python36 path in the current path. Once this is done, `python.exe` can be called from anywhere in the Command Prompt.

Once we invoke the interpreter, the first step to take is to create a variable and assign a value to it.

Python, as with any other programming language, supports various data types for the variables. A data type typically defines the type of value that can be stored in a variable, but Python and PowerShell have the ability to auto-evaluate the type of variable based upon the value. Python supports a large number of data types, but typically in our daily usage we refer to native data types multiple times.

The Python data type supports:

- **Numbers**: These are integer types, such as 1, 2, 100, and 1,000.
- **String**: These are single or multiple characters and possibly every letter of ASCII, such as Python, network, age123, and India. Additionally, a string needs to be stored inside a double quote (") or a single quote (') to specify that a value is a string. Hence, `1` and `'1'` would be interpreted differently by Python.
- **Boolean**: This can be either a true or a false value.
- **Byte**: These are typically binary values.
- **Lists**: These are an ordered sequence of values.
- **Tuples**: These are similar to lists, but the values or length cannot be altered.
- **Sets**: These are similar to lists, but not ordered.

- **Dictionary** or **hash values**: These are key-value pairs, like a telephone directory in which one primary value (name) is attached with both phone numbers and addresses.

An example on data types is as follows:

```
Python 3.6.1 Shell                                                    ─  □  ✕
File  Edit  Shell  Debug  Options  Window  Help
Python 3.6.1 (v3.6.1:69c0db5, Mar 21 2017, 17:54:52) [MSC v.1900 32 bit (Intel)]
 on win32
Type "copyright", "credits" or "license()" for more information.
>>> intvalue=2
>>> intvalue
2
>>> stringvalue='this is a test'
>>> stringvalue
'this is a test'
>>> booleanvalue=True
>>> booleanvalue
True
>>> bytevalue=bytes(3)
>>> bytevalue
b'\x00\x00\x00'
>>>
```

As we can see in the preceding example, we declared the variables with various values, and based upon the value, Python automatically interprets the specific data type. If we just type the variable name again, it prints out the value stored in the variable based upon its data type.

Similarly, the following example specifies other native data types:

```
Python 3.6.1 Shell
File  Edit  Shell  Debug  Options  Window  Help
Python 3.6.1 (v3.6.1:69c0db5, Mar 21 2017, 17:54:52) [MSC v.1900 32 bit (Intel)]
 on win32
Type "copyright", "credits" or "license()" for more information.
>>> listvalue = [1, 2, 3, 4, 5 ]
>>> listvalue
[1, 2, 3, 4, 5]
>>> tuplevalue = ("one", "two")
>>> tuplevalue
('one', 'two')
>>> setvalue = set(["India", "US", "UK"])
>>> setvalue
{'India', 'UK', 'US'}
>>> dictvalue = {'Country': 'India', 'Currency': 'Rupee', 'Capital': 'Delhi'}
>>> dictvalue
{'Country': 'India', 'Currency': 'Rupee', 'Capital': 'Delhi'}
>>> |
```

Additionally, to see the data type we can use the `type()` function, which returns the type of a variable based upon the value we gave. The variable is passed as an argument to the `type()` function to get the data type value:

```
>>> type(listvalue)
<class 'list'>
>>> type(setvalue)
<class 'set'>
>>> type(dictvalue)
<class 'dict'>
>>> type(tuplevalue)
<class 'tuple'>
>>> |
```

A PowerShell example of the same Python code is as follows:

```
#PowerShell code
$value=5
$value="hello"
write-host $value
write-host $value.gettype()
#This is remark
#A variable in powershell is declared with '$' sign in front.
# The gettype() function in powershell is used to get the type of variable.
```

There are operations, such as addition (+), for specific variables with particular data types. We have to be sure what types of variable we are adding. If we have an incompatible data type variable being added to another one, Python would throw an error stating the reason.

Here in the following code, we see the result of adding two string variables:

```
Python 3.6.1 Shell
File  Edit  Shell  Debug  Options  Window  Help
Python 3.6.1 (v3.6.1:69c0db5, Mar 21 2017, 17:54:52) [MSC v.1900 32 bit (Intel)]
 on win32
Type "copyright", "credits" or "license()" for more information.
>>> stringval="1"
>>> stringval
'1'
>>> stringval2="2"
>>> stringval2
'2'
>>> stringval3 =stringval+stringval2
>>> stringval3
'12'
>>>
```

Similarly, observe the difference if we use the same addition on integer variables:

```
Python 3.6.1 Shell
File  Edit  Shell  Debug  Options  Window  Help
Python 3.6.1 (v3.6.1:69c0db5, Mar 21 2017, 17:54:52) [MSC v.1900 32 bit (Intel)]
 on win32
Type "copyright", "credits" or "license()" for more information.
>>> intvalue=1
>>> intvalue
1
>>> intvalue2=2
>>> intvalue3=intvalue+intvalue2
>>> intvalue3
3
>>>
```

As mentioned, let's see what happens when we try to add a string and an integer variable together:

```
Python 3.6.1 Shell
File  Edit  Shell  Debug  Options  Window  Help
Python 3.6.1 (v3.6.1:69c0db5, Mar 21 2017, 17:54:52) [MSC v.1900 32 bit (Intel)]
 on win32
Type "copyright", "credits" or "license()" for more information.
>>> stringvalue='1'
>>> intvalue=2
>>> mixedvalue=stringvalue+intvalue
Traceback (most recent call last):
  File "<pyshell#2>", line 1, in <module>
    mixedvalue=stringvalue+intvalue
TypeError: must be str, not int
>>>
```

The error clearly specifies that we cannot add two different data types because the interpreter cannot recognize which data type needs to be assigned to the mixed value variable.

Sometimes, if necessary, we can convert the values from one data type to another by calling specific functions that convert the data type to another. For example, `int("1")` will convert the string value 1 to integer value 1, or `str(1)` will convert the integer value 1 to the string value 1.

We will be extensively using the various data types depending upon the logic and requirements of the scripts, and also, if necessary, converting one data type to another to achieve certain results.

Conditions and loops

Conditions are checked using a left and right value comparison. The evaluation returns either true or false, and a specific action is performed depending on the result.

There are certain condition operators that are used to evaluate the left and right value comparisons:

Operators	Meaning
==	If both values are equal
!=	If both values are NOT equal

>	If the left value is greater than the right value
<	If the left value is smaller than the right value
>=	If the left value is greater than or equal to the right value
<=	If the left value is lesser than or equal to the right value
in	If the left value is part of the right value

An example of the condition evaluation is as follows:

```
Python 3.6.1 Shell                                                    [ _ ][ □ ][ X ]
File  Edit  Shell  Debug  Options  Window  Help
Python 3.6.1 (v3.6.1:69c0db5, Mar 21 2017, 17:54:52) [MSC v.1900 32 bit (Intel)]
 on win32
Type "copyright", "credits" or "license()" for more information.
>>> if 2>3:
        print ("left value is greater")
else:
        print ("right value is greater")


right value is greater
>>>
```

As we can see, we are checking whether 2>3 (2 is greater that 3). Of course, this would result in false, so the action in the `else` section is executed. If we reverse the check, 3>2, then the output would have been `left value is greater`.

In the preceding example, we used the `if` condition block, which consists of the following:

```
if <condition>:
perform action
else:
perform action2
```

Notice the indentation, which is compulsory in Python. If we had not intended it, Python would not interpret what action to execute in which condition, and hence would have thrown an error of incorrect indentation.

Nested and multiple conditions

Sometimes we need to check multiple conditions in a single `if` condition.

Let's see an example of this:

```
marks=85
if marks <= 45:
    print ("Grade C")
elif marks > 45 and marks <= 75:
    print ("Grade B")
elif marks > 75:
    print ("Grade A")
else:
    print ("Unable to determine")
```

```
Python 3.6.1 (v3.6.1:69c0db5, Mar 21 2017, 17:54:52) [MSC v.1900 32 bit (Intel)]
 on win32
Type "copyright", "credits" or "license()" for more information.
>>>
===================== RESTART: C:/a1/nestedcondition.py =====================
Grade A
>>>
```

Here, we are checking the range of the marks. The flow of the program is as follows:

Assign a value of 85 to the `marks` variable. If `marks` is less than or equal to 45, print Grade C, else if `marks` is greater than 45 and less than equal to 75, print Grade B, else if `marks` is greater than 75, print Grade A, else if none of the preceding conditions match, then print Unable to determine.

The PowerShell sample code for the preceding Python task is as follows:

```
#PowerShell sample code:
$marks=85
if ($marks -le 45)
{
    write-host "Grade C"
}
```

```
elseif (($marks -gt 45) -and ($marks -le 75))
{
    write-host "Grade B"
}
elseif ($marks -gt 75)
{
    write-host "Grade A"
}
else
{
    write-host "Unable to determine"
}
```

Similarly, here is an example of a nested condition (note the indentation that differentiates it from the earlier example of multiple conditions):

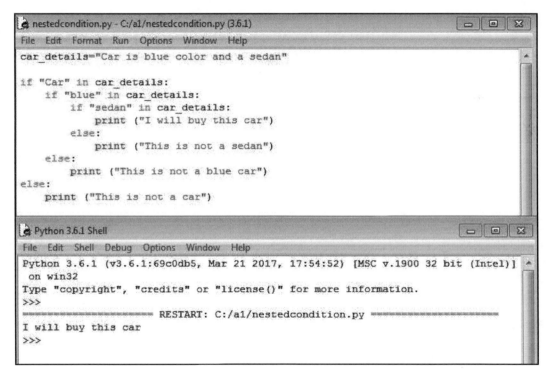

As we can see in the condition, the internal conditions will only be executed if its parent condition evaluates to true. If there is a false, the corresponding else action will be taken. In the example, if the car_details variable contains Car, contains blue, and it contains sedan, only then will the action I will buy this car be performed. If any of those conditions are not met, the relevant else action will be performed.

Loops

A loop is used to repeat a set of instructions until a specific condition is fulfilled. There are two common ways of creating a loop in Python, which are discussed as follows:

For next loop

This type of loop checks for a condition and repeats the instructions inside the loop until the condition is met:

```
for <incremental variable> in final value:
    statements
```

Here's an example of printing numbers from 1 to 10 in a for loop:

```
Python 3.6.1 Shell                                              □  ▣  ☒

File  Edit  Shell  Debug  Options  Window  Help

Python 3.6.1 (v3.6.1:69c0db5, Mar 21 2017, 17:54:52) [MSC v.1900 32 bit (Intel)]
 on win32
Type "copyright", "credits" or "license()" for more information.
>>> for x in range(1,10):
        print (x)


1
2
3
4
5
6
7
8
9
>>>
```

As we can see, we use a built-in `range(starting value, max value)` function, which specifies the loop to repeat from the starting value until the incremental value reaches the maximum value. In this case, the variable x is incremented by 1 and in each loop, the value is printed out. This is repeated until the value of x reaches 10, where the for loop terminates.

In a similar way, we can also iterate through the items in a given list:

```
Python 3.6.1 Shell
File  Edit  Shell  Debug  Options  Window  Help
Python 3.6.1 (v3.6.1:69c0db5, Mar 21 2017, 17:54:52) [MSC v.1900 32 bit (Intel)]
 on win32
Type "copyright", "credits" or "license()" for more information.
>>> countries=['India','UK','USA','France']
>>> for country in countries:
        print (country + " is good")


India is good
UK is good
USA is good
France is good
>>>
```

PowerShell sample for the preceding Python code is as follows:

```
#PowerShell sample code:
$countries="India","UK","USA","France"
foreach ($country in $countries)
{
    write-host ($country+" is good")
}
```

Here, we can see that the values are assigned to the countries variable as a list. The `for` loop now iterates through each item in the list, and the print statement adds the string value to another string value and prints the result. This loop is repeated until all the items in the list are printed.

There might be times when we do not want to parse through an entire `for` loop. To break from the loop while it is iterating, we use a `break` statement. Here's an example in which we want to stop printing after UK in the `country` list:

```
for country in countries:
    if 'UK' in country:
        break
    else:
        print (country)
```

While loop

While loop is different from for loop, as no new variable is needed in this loop, and any current variable can be used to perform the tasks inside the while loop. An example is as follows:

```
while True:
    perform instructions
    if condition():
      break
```

```
Python 3.6.1 Shell
File  Edit  Shell  Debug  Options  Window  Help
Python 3.6.1 (v3.6.1:69c0db5, Mar 21 2017, 17:54:52) [MSC v.1900 32 bit (Intel)]
on win32
Type "copyright", "credits" or "license()" for more information.
>>> x=1
>>> while True:
        print (x)
        if x>=10:
                break
        x=x+1


1
2
3
4
5
6
7
8
9
10
>>>
```

This is similar to for, but in this case the actions are performed first, and then the condition is checked. In the preceding example, the value of x is printed first, and we repeat the same set of instructions until the value of x reaches 10 or greater. Once the if condition is met, we break out of the loop. If we do not specify a break condition, we will go into an infinite loop with a increment of 1 for each x value.

Writing Python scripts

We are now familiar with the basic concepts of Python. Now we will write an actual program or script in Python.

Ask for the input of a country name, and check whether the last character of the country is a vowel:

```python
countryname=input("Enter country name:")
countryname=countryname.lower()
lastcharacter=countryname.strip()[-1]
if 'a' in lastcharacter:
    print ("Vowel found")
elif 'e' in lastcharacter:
    print ("Vowel found")
elif 'i' in lastcharacter:
    print ("Vowel found")
elif 'o' in lastcharacter:
    print ("Vowel found")
elif 'u' in lastcharacter:
    print ("Vowel found")
else:
    print ("No vowel found")
```

Output of the preceding code is as follows:

```
Python 3.6.1 Shell                                            _  □  ☒
File  Edit  Shell  Debug  Options  Window  Help
Python 3.6.1 (v3.6.1:69c0db5, Mar 21 2017, 17:54:52) [MSC v.1900 32 bit (Intel)]
 on win32
Type "copyright", "credits" or "license()" for more information.
>>>
==================== RESTART: C:/a1/book/checkvowel.py ====================
Enter country name:India
Vowel found
>>>
==================== RESTART: C:/a1/book/checkvowel.py ====================
Enter country name:UK
No vowel found
>>>
==================== RESTART: C:/a1/book/checkvowel.py ====================
Enter country name:USA
Vowel found
>>>
```

1. We ask for the input of a country name. The `input()` method is used to get an input from the user. The value entered is in the string format, and in our case the `countryname` variable has been assigned the input value.

2. In the next line, `countryname.lower()` specifies that the input that we receive needs to converted into all lowercase and stored in the same `countryname` variable. This effectively will have the same value that we entered earlier but in lowercase.

3. In the next line, `countryname.strip()[-1]` specifies two actions in one statement:

   - `countryname.strip()` ensures that the variable has all the leading and trailing extra values removed, such as new line or tab characters.
   - Once we get the clean variable, remove the last character of the string, which in our case is the last character of the country name. The `-1` denotes the character from right to left or end to start, whereas +1 would denote from left to right.

4. Once we have the last character stored in the `lastcharacter` variable, all that is needed is a nested condition check and, based upon the result, print the value.

To save this program, we need to save this file as `somename.py`, which will specify that this program needs to be executed in Python:

The PowerShell sample code for the preceding Python task is as follows:

```
#PowerShell sample code
$countryname=read-host "Enter country name"
$countryname=$countryname.tolower()
$lastcharacter=$countryname[-1]
if ($lastcharacter -contains 'a')
{
    write-host "Vowel found"
}
elseif ($lastcharacter -contains 'e')
{
    write-host "Vowel found"
}
elseif ($lastcharacter -contains 'i')
{
    write-host "Vowel found"
}
elseif ($lastcharacter -contains 'o')
```

```
{
    write-host "Vowel found"
}
elseif ($lastcharacter -contains 'u')
{
    write-host "Vowel found"
}
else
{
write-host "No vowel found"
}
```

 Python is very strict in terms of indentation. As we can see in the example, if we change the indentations or tabs even by a space, Python will spit out an error stating the indentation is not correct and the compilation will fail. This will result in an error and unless the indentation is fixed, the execution will not be performed.

Functions

For any recurring set of instructions, we can define a function. In other words, a function is a closed set of instructions to perform a specific logic or task. Depending upon the input provided, a function has the ability to return the results or parse the input with specific instructions to get results without any return values.

A function is defined by the def keyword, which specifies that we need to define a function and provide a set of instructions related to that function.

In this task we will print the greater of two input numbers:

```
def checkgreaternumber(number1,number2):
    if number1 > number2:
      print ("Greater number is ",number1)
    else:
      print ("Greater number is",number2)
checkgreaternumber(2,4)
checkgreaternumber(3,1)
```

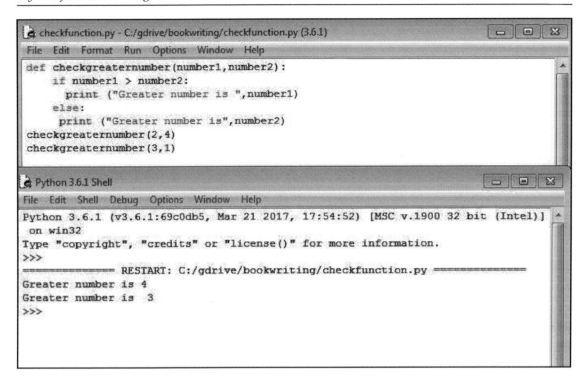

As we can see in the preceding output, the first time we call the `checkgreaternumber(2,4)` function, the function prints the greater value as 4, and the second time we call the function with different numbers, the function prints the greater value as 3.

The PowerShell sample code for the preceding task is as follows:

```
#PowerShell sample code
function checkgreaternumber($number1,$number2)
{
    if ($number1 -gt $number2)
    {
        write-host ("Greater number is "+$number1)
    }
    else
    {
        write-host ("Greater number is "+$number2)
    }
}

checkgreaternumber 2 4
checkgreaternumber 3 1
```

We can rewrite the same function, but rather than printing the value inside the function, it should return the greater number:

```
def checkgreaternumber(number1,number2):
    if number1 > number2:
      return number1
    else:
     return number2


print ("My greater number in 2 and 4 is ",checkgreaternumber(2,4))
print ("My greater number in 3 and 1 is ",checkgreaternumber(3,1))
```

In this case, as we can see, the function returns the value, and the result is returned on the line where the function was called. In this case, as it was called inside the print function, it evaluates the input and returns the value, which also gets printed out inside the same print function.

```
#PowerShell sample code
function checkgreaternumber($number1,$number2)
{
    if ($number1 -gt $number2)
    {
        return $number1
    }
    else
    {
        return $number2
    }
}

write-host ("My greater number in 2 and 4 is ",(checkgreaternumber 2 4))
write-host ("My greater number in 3 and 1 is ",(checkgreaternumber 3 1))
```

Another important aspect of a function is the default values that we can provide in a function. Sometimes we need to write functions that might take multiple, say 4, 5, or more, values as inputs. Since it becomes hard to know what values we need and in which order for the function, we can ensure that the default value is taken into consideration if any value is not provided when calling that specific function:

```
def checkgreaternumber(number1,number2=5):
    if number1 > number2:
      return number1
    else:
     return number2
print ("Greater value is",checkgreaternumber(3))
print ("Greater value is",checkgreaternumber(6))
print ("Greater value is",checkgreaternumber(1,4))
```

The output of the code execution is given as:

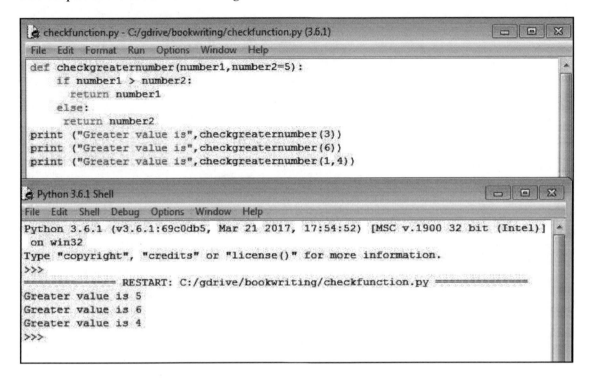

1. As we can see in the preceding output, we specified the default value of number2 as 5. Now, as we can see in the first call to the function, we only give the value 3. Now, as the function needs two inputs or parameters, but we provided only one, the second value for the function is taken from the default one, which is 5 in this case. Hence, a comparison will be done between 3 and 5 to get the greater number.

2. In the second call to the function, a similar call is made with 6, and since no other value was provided, the comparison was between 6 and 5, and result returned was the greater value, which is 6.

3. In the third call, we provide both values, which overrides any default value, so a comparison was done between 1 and 4. The result was evaluated and the output of 4 was returned.

Another important consideration is the localization of a variable in a function:

```
globalval=6

def checkglobalvalue():
    return globalval

def localvariablevalue():
    globalval=8
    return globalval

print ("This is global value",checkglobalvalue())
print ("This is global value",globalval)
print ("This is local value",localvariablevalue())
print ("This is global value",globalval)
```

The output of the preceding code is as follows:

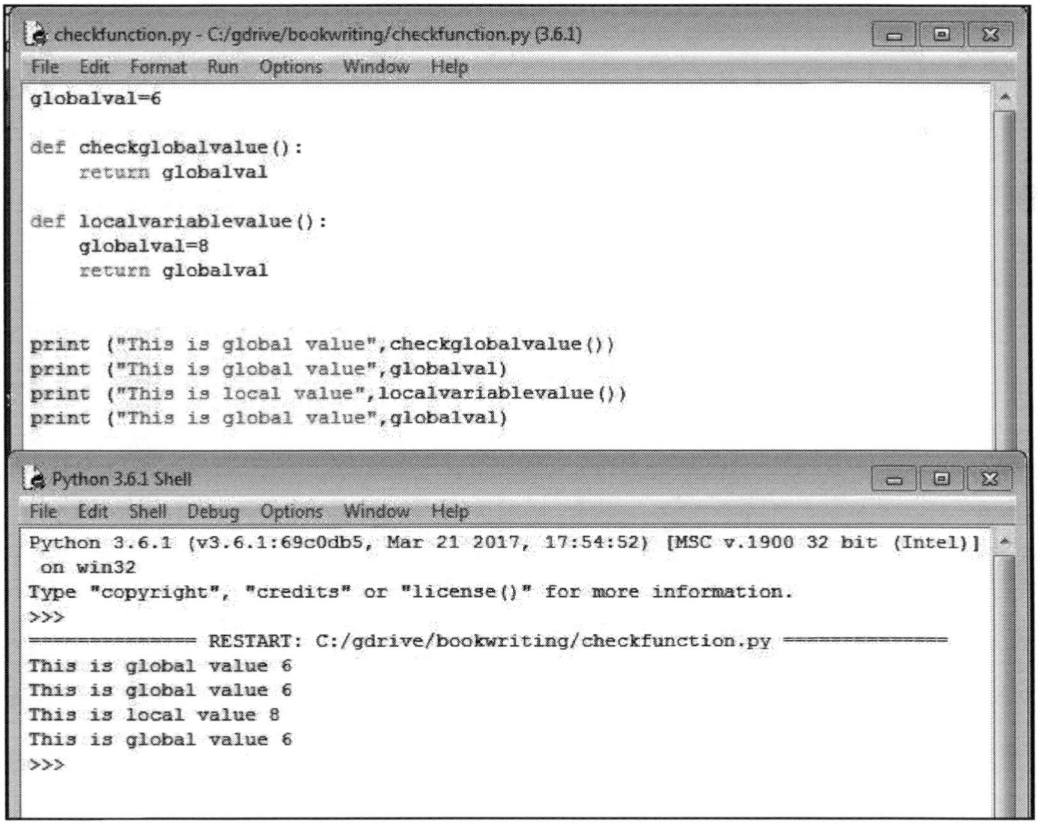

1. In the preceding output, we define a variable named as `globalval` with a value of 6. In the `checkglobalvalue` function, we just return the value of the `globalvalvariable`, which prints a value of 6 as we call the first `print` function.

2. The second `print` function just prints the value of the same variable, which also prints 6.

3. Now, in the third `print` function, `localvariablevalue`, we call the same `globalval`, but give it a value of 8 and return the value of `globalval`. In the print value of local, it prints the result as value 8. It is not assumed that the `globalval` variable has a value of 8 now. But, as we can see in the last `print` function, it still prints a value of 6, when we call the `print` function to print the value of `globalval`.

This clearly shows that any variable inside a function is locally effective, or is localized, but does not have any impact on any variables outside the function. We need to use the `global` command to reference the global variable and remove the localization impact of it.

Here is the same example before using the `global` command:

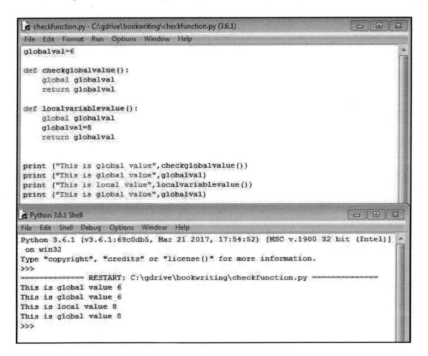

As can we see in the preceding output, if we change the value of the globalval global variable inside the localvariablevalue function, we see the effect on the global variable with a new value of 8.

Passing arguments from the command line

Sometimes it is necessary to pass arguments to the script from the command line. This is generally needed when we need to perform some quick actions in our script, rather than the script asking us for the inputs.

Consider the following lines of code where we pass two numbers as arguments to scripts, and print the sum of them:

```
import sys
print ("Total output is ")
print (int(sys.argv[1])+int(sys.argv[2]))
```

When we run this script, say it's saved as checkargs.py, and execute it as follows:

```
python checkargs.py 5 6
```

The output returned is as follows:

```
Total output is
11
```

The key here is the import of the sys module, which is a predefined module in Python to handle any system-related tasks of Python. The values that we pass as arguments are stored in sys.argv[1] onwards, since sys.argv[0] is the name of actual script being run. In this case, sys.argv[0] will be checkargs.py, sys.argv[1] will be 5, and sys.argv[2] will be 6.

The PowerShell code for the preceding task is as follows:

```
#PowerShell sample code
$myvalue=$args[0]
write-host ("Argument passed to PowerShell is "+$myvalue)
```

The arguments passed in a Python script are in string format, so we need to explicitly convert them to the right type for the expected output. In the preceding script, if we had not converted it to the integer type by using the int() function, then the output would have been 56 instead of int(5) + int(6) = 11.

Python modules and packages

Because Python is the most popular open source coding language, there are many developers who contribute their expertise by creating specific modules and sharing them for others to use. These modules are a specific set of functions or instructions that are used to perform specialized tasks and can be called easily in our programs. The modules can be easily called using the `import` command inside the scripts. Python has many built-in modules that are directly called using `import`, but for specialized modules, an external installation is needed. Luckily, Python provides a very easy way to download and install these modules.

As an example, let's install a module named `Netmiko` that can help us work on logging into network devices more efficiently. Python provides a well-documented reference for each of the modules, and for our module, the documentation can be found at `https://pypi.python.org/pypi/netmiko`. For installation, all we have to do is go into the folder from the command line where `python.exe` is installed or is present. There is a sub folder in that location called `scripts`.

Inside that folder, we have two options that can be used for installing modules, `easy_install.exe` or `pip.exe`.

Installing the library for Python, can be done in two ways:

- The syntax of `easy_install` is as follows:

      easy_install <name of module>

  For example:

      easy_install netmiko

- The syntax of `pip install` is as follows:

      pip install <name of module>

  For example:

      pip install netmiko

Once we install the required module, we need to restart Python by closing all open sessions and invoking IDLE again so the modules can be loaded. More information on modules can be gathered from `https://docs.python.org/2/tutorial/modules.html`.

Multithreading for parallel processing

As we are now focusing on writing our scripts efficiently, a major aspect of this is how efficiently, quickly, and correctly we fetch the information. When we use the `for` loop, we parse through each item one by one, which is fine if we get results quickly.

Now, if each item in a `for` loop is a router from which we need to get the output of show version, and if each router takes around 10 seconds to log in, gather the output, and log out, and we have around 30 routers that we need to get this information from, we would need 10*30 = 300 seconds for the program to complete the execution. If we are looking for more advanced or complex calculations on each output, which might take up to a minute, then it will take 30 minutes for just 30 routers.

This starts becoming very inefficient when our complexity and scalability grows. To help with this, we need to add parallelism to our programs. What this simply means is, we log in simultaneously on all 30 routers, and perform the same task to fetch the output at the same time. Effectively, this means that we now get the output on all 30 routers in 10 seconds, because we have 30 parallel threads being called.

A thread is nothing but another instance of the same function being called, and calling it 30 times means we are invoking 30 threads at the same time to perform the same tasks.

Here's an example:

```python
import datetime
from threading import Thread

def checksequential():
    for x in range(1,10):
        print (datetime.datetime.now().time())

def checkparallel():
    print (str(datetime.datetime.now().time())+"\n")

checksequential()
print ("\nNow printing parallel threads\n")
threads = []
for x in range(1,10):
    t = Thread(target=checkparallel)
    t.start()
    threads.append(t)

for t in threads:
    t.join()
```

The output of the multi-threading code is as follows:

1. As we can see in the preceding example, we created two functions, named `checksequential` and `checkparallel`, to print the system's date time. The `datetime` module is used to get the system's date time in this case. In the `for` loop, a sequential run was done that shows the increment time in the output when the function was called.

2. For the threading, we use a blank array named `threads`. Each of the instances that is created has a unique thread number or value, which is stored in this empty thread array each time the `checkparallel` method is spawned. This unique number or reference for each thread identifies each thread as and when its executed. The `start()` method is used to get the thread to perform the function called in the thread.

3. The last loop is important in the thread. What it signifies is that the program will wait for all the threads to complete before moving forward. The `join()` method specifies that until all the threads are complete, the program will not proceed to the next step.

Now, as we can see in the output of the thread, some of the timestamps are the same, which means that all those instances were invoked and executed at the same time in parallel rather than sequentially.

The output in the program is not in order for parallel threads, because the moment any thread is completed, the output is printed, irrespective of the order. This is different to sequential execution, since parallel threads do not wait for any previous thread to complete before executing another. So, any thread that completes will print its value and end.

PowerShell sample code for the preceding task is as follows:

```
#PowerShell sample code
Get-Job   #This get the current running threads or Jobs in PowerShell
Remove-Job -Force * # This commands closes forcible all the previous
threads

$Scriptblock = {
    Param (
        [string]$ipaddress
    )
    if (Test-Connection $ipaddress -quiet)
    {
        return ("Ping for "+$ipaddress+" is successful")
    }
    else
    {
        return ("Ping for "+$ipaddress+" FAILED")
    }
}

$iplist="4.4.4.4","8.8.8.8","10.10.10.10","20.20.20.20","4.2.2.2"

foreach ($ip in $iplist)
```

```
{
    Start-Job -ScriptBlock $Scriptblock -ArgumentList $ip | Out-Null
    #The above command is used to invoke the $scriptblock in a multithread
}

#Following logic waits for all the threads or Jobs to get completed
While (@(Get-Job | Where { $_.State -eq "Running" }).Count -ne 0)
  { # Write-Host "Waiting for background jobs..."
    Start-Sleep -Seconds 1
  }

#Following logic is used to print all the values that are returned by each
thread and then remove the thread # #or job from memory
ForEach ($Job in (Get-Job)) {
  Receive-Job $Job
  Remove-Job $Job
  }
```

Using Netmiko for SSH and network device interaction

Netmiko (`https://github.com/ktbyers/netmiko`) is a library in Python that is used extensively an interaction with network devices. This is a multi-vendor library with support for Cisco IOS, NXOS, firewalls, and many other devices. The underlying library of this is Paramiko, which is again used extensively for SSH into various devices.

Netmiko extends the Paramiko ability of SSH to add enhancements, such as going into configuration mode in network routers, sending commands, receiving output based upon the commands, adding enhancements to wait for certain commands to finish executing, and also taking care of yes/no prompts during command execution.

Here's an example of a simple script to log in to the router and show the version:

```
from netmiko import ConnectHandler

device = ConnectHandler(device_type='cisco_ios', ip='192.168.255.249',
username='cisco', password='cisco')
output = device.send_command("show version")
print (output)
device.disconnect()
```

The output of the execution of code against a router is as follows:

As we can see in the sample code, we call the `ConnectHandler` function from the Netmiko library, which takes four inputs (`platform type`, `IP address of device`, `username`, and `password`):

Netmiko works with a variety of vendors. Some of the supported platform types and their abbreviations to be called in Netmiko are:

'a10': A10SSH,
'accedian': AccedianSSH,
'alcatel_aos': AlcatelAosSSH,
'alcatel_sros': AlcatelSrosSSH,
'arista_eos': AristaSSH,
'aruba_os': ArubaSSH,
'avaya_ers': AvayaErsSSH,
'avaya_vsp': AvayaVspSSH,
'brocade_fastiron': BrocadeFastironSSH,
'brocade_netiron': BrocadeNetironSSH,
'brocade_nos': BrocadeNosSSH,
'brocade_vdx': BrocadeNosSSH,
'brocade_vyos': VyOSSSH,
'checkpoint_gaia': CheckPointGaiaSSH,
'ciena_saos': CienaSaosSSH,
'cisco_asa': CiscoAsaSSH,
'cisco_ios': CiscoIosBase,
'cisco_nxos': CiscoNxosSSH,
'cisco_s300': CiscoS300SSH,
'cisco_tp': CiscoTpTcCeSSH,
'cisco_wlc': CiscoWlcSSH,
'cisco_xe': CiscoIosBase,
'cisco_xr': CiscoXrSSH,
'dell_force10': DellForce10SSH,
'dell_powerconnect': DellPowerConnectSSH,
'eltex': EltexSSH,
'enterasys': EnterasysSSH,
'extreme': ExtremeSSH,
'extreme_wing': ExtremeWingSSH,
'f5_ltm': F5LtmSSH,
'fortinet': FortinetSSH,
'generic_termserver': TerminalServerSSH,
'hp_comware': HPComwareSSH,
'hp_procurve': HPProcurveSSH,

'huawei': HuaweiSSH,
'juniper': JuniperSSH,
'juniper_junos': JuniperSSH,
'linux': LinuxSSH,
'mellanox_ssh': MellanoxSSH,
'mrv_optiswitch': MrvOptiswitchSSH,
'ovs_linux': OvsLinuxSSH,
'paloalto_panos': PaloAltoPanosSSH,
'pluribus': PluribusSSH,
'quanta_mesh': QuantaMeshSSH,
'ubiquiti_edge': UbiquitiEdgeSSH,
'vyatta_vyos': VyOSSSH,
'vyos': VyOSSSH,

Depending upon the selection of the platform type, Netmiko can understand the returned prompt and the correct way to SSH to the specific device. Once the connection is made, we can send commands to the device using the `send` method.

Once we get the return value, the value stored in the `output` variable is displayed, which is the string output of the command that we sent to the device. The last line, which uses the `disconnect` function, ensures that the connection is terminated cleanly once we are done with our task.

For configuration (example: We need to provide a description to the router interface `FastEthernet 0/0`), we use Netmiko as shown in the following example:

```
from netmiko import ConnectHandler

print ("Before config push")
device = ConnectHandler(device_type='cisco_ios', ip='192.168.255.249',
username='cisco', password='cisco')
output = device.send_command("show running-config interface fastEthernet
0/0")
print (output)

configcmds=["interface fastEthernet 0/0", "description my test"]
device.send_config_set(configcmds)

print ("After config push")
output = device.send_command("show running-config interface fastEthernet
0/0")
print (output)

device.disconnect()
```

The output of the execution of the preceding code is as follows:

```
Python 3.6.1 Shell                                              [_][▢][✕]
File  Edit  Shell  Debug  Options  Window  Help
Python 3.6.1 (v3.6.1:69c0db5, Mar 21 2017, 17:54:52) [MSC v.1900 32 bit (Intel)]
 on win32
Type "copyright", "credits" or "license()" for more information.
>>>
========================= RESTART: C:/a1/checknetmiko.py =========================
Before config push
Building configuration...

Current configuration : 102 bytes
!
interface FastEthernet0/0
 ip address 192.168.255.249 255.255.255.252
 duplex auto
 speed auto
end

After config push
Building configuration...

Current configuration : 123 bytes
!
interface FastEthernet0/0
 description my test
 ip address 192.168.255.249 255.255.255.252
 duplex auto
 speed auto
end

>>>
```

- As we can see, for `config push` we do not have to perform any additional configs but just specify the commands in the same order as we will send them manually to the router in a list, and pass that list as an argument to the `send_config_set` function.
- The output in `Before config push` is a simple output of the `FastEthernet0/0` interface, but the output under `After config push` is now with the description that we configured using the list of commands.

In a similar way, we can pass multiple commands to the router, and Netmiko will go into configuration mode, write those commands to the router, and exit config mode.

If we want to save the configuration, we use the following command after the `send_config_set` command:

```
device.send_command("write memory")
```

This ensures that the router writes the newly pushed config in memory.

Network automation use case

As we have now interacted with multiple sections of Python and device interaction, let's create a use case to incorporate what we have learned so far. The use case is as follows:

Log into the router and fetch some information:

1. `task1()`: Show the version, show the IP in brief, show the clock, and show the configured usernames on the router.
2. `task2()`: Create another username on the `test` router with the password `test` and check whether we can log in successfully with the newly created username.
3. `task3()`: Log in with the newly created username `test`, and delete all the other usernames from the `running-config`. Once this is done, return all the current usernames configured on the router to confirm whether only the `test` username is configured on the router.

Let's build a script to tackle these tasks one by one:

```
from netmiko import ConnectHandler

device = ConnectHandler(device_type='cisco_ios', ip='192.168.255.249',
username='cisco', password='cisco')

def task1():
    output = device.send_command("show version")
    print (output)
    output= device.send_command("show ip int brief")
    print (output)
    output= device.send_command("show clock")
    print (output)
    output= device.send_command("show running-config | in username")
    output=output.splitlines()
    for item in output:
        if ("username" in item):
            item=item.split(" ")
            print ("username configured: ",item[1])
```

```
def task2():
    global device
    configcmds=["username test privilege 15 secret test"]
    device.send_config_set(configcmds)
    output= device.send_command("show running-config | in username")
    output=output.splitlines()
    for item in output:
        if ("username" in item):
            item=item.split(" ")
            print ("username configured: ",item[1])
    device.disconnect()
    try:
        device = ConnectHandler(device_type='cisco_ios',
ip='192.168.255.249', username='test', password='test')
        print ("Authenticated successfully with username test")
        device.disconnect()
    except:
        print ("Unable to authenticate with username test")

def task3():
    device = ConnectHandler(device_type='cisco_ios', ip='192.168.255.249',
username='test', password='test')
    output= device.send_command("show running-config | in username")
    output=output.splitlines()
    for item in output:
        if ("username" in item):
            if ("test" not in item):
                item=item.split(" ")
                cmd="no username "+item[1]
                outputnew=device.send_config_set(cmd)
    output= device.send_command("show running-config | in username")
    output=output.splitlines()
    for item in output:
        if ("username" in item):
            item=item.split(" ")
            print ("username configured: ",item[1])
    device.disconnect()
#Call task1 by writing task1()
#task1()
#Call task2 by writing task2()
#task2()
#Call task3 by writing task3()
#task3()
```

As we can see, the three tasks given are defined as three different functions:

1. The first line indicates that we have imported the Netmiko library, and in the second line we are connecting to our `test` router with the Cisco credentials.

2. In the `task1()` function, we are fetching the outputs of all show commands. Additionally, since we do not want to expose the passwords of the current usernames we have added an extra logic wherein the returned output for `show running-config | in username` will be parsed by each line for every username, and each line will be split by a space character " ". Also, since the Cisco device returns the actual username in the second position in the output (for example, username `test` privilege 15 secret 5), we print the value of the second item after we split the output string, which is our actual username.

Here's the output for the `task1()` method:

```
This product contains cryptographic features and is subject to United
States and local country laws governing import, export, transfer and
use. Delivery of Cisco cryptographic products does not imply
third-party authority to import, export, distribute or use encryption.
Importers, exporters, distributors and users are responsible for
compliance with U.S. and local country laws. By using this product you
agree to comply with applicable laws and regulations. If you are unable
to comply with U.S. and local laws, return this product immediately.

A summary of U.S. laws governing Cisco cryptographic products may be found at:
http://www.cisco.com/wwl/export/crypto/tool/stqrg.html

If you require further assistance please contact us by sending email to
export@cisco.com.

Cisco 3745 (R7000) processor (revision 2.0) with 249856K/12288K bytes of memory.
Processor board ID FTX0945W0MY
R7000 CPU at 350MHz, Implementation 39, Rev 2.1, 256KB L2, 512KB L3 Cache
3 FastEthernet interfaces
1 Serial(sync/async) interface
DRAM configuration is 64 bits wide with parity enabled.
151K bytes of NVRAM.

Configuration register is 0x2102

Interface              IP-Address       OK? Method Status                Protocol
FastEthernet0/0        192.168.255.249  YES NVRAM  up                    up
Serial0/0              unassigned       YES NVRAM  administratively down  down
FastEthernet0/1        unassigned       YES NVRAM  administratively down  down
FastEthernet1/0        unassigned       YES NVRAM  administratively down  down
*00:26:48.907 UTC Fri Mar 1 2002
username configured:  cisco
>>>
```

3. In the `task2()` method, we are going to create a username `test` with the password `test`, and authenticate with the new username. We have added a `try:` exception block in this method, which checks for any errors/exceptions for all the statements in the `try:` section, and if there are any exceptions, rather than breaking the script, it runs the code that is given in the exception section (under the `except:` keyword). If there are no errors, it continues with the statements in the `try:` section.

   Here's the output for `task2()`:

```
Python 3.6.1 Shell
File  Edit  Shell  Debug  Options  Window  Help
Python 3.6.1 (v3.6.1:69c0db5, Mar 21 2017, 17:54:52) [MSC v.1900 32 bit (Intel)]
 on win32
Type "copyright", "credits" or "license()" for more information.
>>>
======================= RESTART: C:\a1\checknetmiko.py =======================
username configured:  cisco
username configured:  test
Authenticated successfully with username test
>>>
```

   We can see that we now have two usernames configured, and the router is also now successfully responding to authentication with the `test` username.

4. In `task3()` function, this will first fetch all the usernames that are in `running-config`, and if there are any usernames that are not `test`, it will create a dynamic command with no username `<username>` and send it to the router. Once it is done with all the usernames, it will go ahead and recheck and list out all the usernames not on the router. A success criteria is only the configured username as `test` should be available on the router.

Here's the output of `task3()`:

```
Python 3.6.1 Shell                                          □ □ ▨
File  Edit  Shell  Debug  Options  Window  Help
Python 3.6.1 (v3.6.1:69c0db5, Mar 21 2017, 17:54:52) [MSC v.1900 32 bit (Intel)]
 on win32
Type "copyright", "credits" or "license()" for more information.
>>>
========================= RESTART: C:\a1\checknetmiko.py =========================
username configured:   test
>>>
```

The result of `task3()` is the result of all configured usernames, which in this case is now only test.

Summary

In this chapter, we learned some advanced techniques for writing scripts by using functions, conditions, and loops; we covered multi-threading our scripts for faster and parallel execution, we got familiar with using Netmiko to interact with network devices, and looked at a real-world example of achieving a certain set of tasks using a single script.

The next chapter will focus on automation tasks using web. We will also discuss how to call Python scripts from the web and perform tasks using web framework.

Additionally, there will be a basic introduction to creating your own API so that others can use it for specific tasks.

3
Accessing and Mining Data from Network

Looking back, we now have a fair idea of the basics of writing Python scripts and how to get meaningful data out of information. We have covered how to write Python scripts, interact with network devices, and have also worked on the basics of PowerShell so that we can work with both PowerShell and Python scripts. Now we will move towards a deeper understanding of using Python by looking at various examples. In this chapter we will focus on working with various Network devices to dig or fetch relevant information from devices, working on that information to create new configurations and pushing it back to the devices for added or enhanced functionality.

We will work on some common scenarios that we may face and try to solve them with Python. These examples or scenarios can be extended depending on a programmer's needs, and can be used as a reference to achieve automation in complex tasks.

Some of the key concepts we will be covering are as follows:

- Device configuration
- Multi-vendor environments
- IPv4 to IPv6 conversion
- Office/DC relocations
- Site rollouts
- BYOD configs for switches
- Device OS upgrades
- IP configs/interface parsing

Device configurations

We need to deploy three routers with a standard base configuration. The base configuration remains the same on each router, but as each router is different, we need to automate the generation of the three config files for each router. The assumption is that all the routers have a standard hardware configuration with the same types of ports:

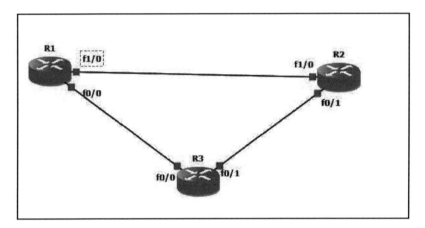

As we can see in the diagram, routers R1, R2, and R3 have the following cabling:

- R1 f1/0 (FastEthernet1/0) connected R2 f1/0
- R1 f0/0 connected to R3 f0/0
- R2 f0/1 connected to R3 f0/1

The standard config or template is as follows:

```
hostname <hname>
ip domain-lookup
ip name-server <nameserver>
logging host <loghost>
username cisco privilege 15 password cisco
enable password cisco
ip domain-name checkmetest.router
line vty 0 4
exec-timeout 5
```

Adding some more complexity, we need to ensure the name-server is different for each router. If each router is going to be deployed in different networks, here is the mapping that we want:

- R1 -> hostname testindia
- R2 -> hostname testusa
- R3 -> hostname testUK

The logging host and name server will depend upon the region, so the mapping will be as follows:

- **India router**: logserver (1.1.1.1) and nameserver (1.1.1.2)
- **USA router**: logserver (2.1.1.1) and nameserver (2.1.1.2)
- **UK router**: logserver (3.1.1.1) and nameserver (3.1.1.2)

The code to perform the requested task is as follows:

```
ipdict={'india': '1.1.1.1,1.1.1.2', 'uk': '3.1.1.1,3.1.1.2', 'usa':
'2.1.1.1,2.1.1.2'}

standardtemplate="""
hostname <hname>
ip domain-lookup
ip name-server <nameserver>
logging host <loghost>
username cisco privilege 15 password cisco
enable password cisco
ip domain-name checkmetest.router

line vty 0 4
 exec-timeout 5
"""

routerlist="R1,R2,R3"
routers=routerlist.split(",")
for router in routers:
print ("Now printing config for",router)
    if "R1" in router:
        hostname="testindia"
        getips=ipdict["india"]
        getips=getips.split(",")
        logserver=getips[0]
        nameserver=getips[1]
    if "R2" in router:
        hostname="testusa"
        getips=ipdict["usa"]
```

```
        getips=getips.split(",")
        logserver=getips[0]
        nameserver=getips[1]
    if "R3" in router:
        hostname="testUK"
        getips=ipdict["uk"]
        getips=getips.split(",")
        logserver=getips[0]
        nameserver=getips[1]
    generatedconfig=standardtemplate
    generatedconfig=generatedconfig.replace("<hname>",hostname)
    generatedconfig=generatedconfig.replace("<nameserver>",nameserver)
    generatedconfig=generatedconfig.replace("<loghost>",logserver)
    print (generatedconfig)
```

The first list is a dictionary that defines the logging host and nameserver config based upon the region. The `standardtemplate` variable is used to store the template. If we have a multi-line value that needs to be stored in a variable, we can use the three-quote format as we see in the preceding example.

Now, as we currently know the generic or default hostnames, we can just parse through each of the current hostnames, and, based upon the hostname values, generate the config. This output can be saved onto a file or can be directly generated from the script and pasted onto the router for the basic configuration. Similarly, we can enhance this by adding the IP addresses shown in the next example in the format `<ipaddress> <subnet mask>`:

- testindia f1/0: `10.0.0.1 255.0.0.0`
- testusa f1/0: `10.0.0.2 255.0.0.0`
- testindia f0/0: `11.0.0.1 255.0.0.0`
- testUK f0/0: `11.0.0.2 255.0.0.0`
- testusa f0/1: `12.0.0.1 255.0.0.0`
- testUK f0/1: `12.0.0.2 255.0.0.0`

The code to perform this task is as follows:

```
def getipaddressconfig(routername):
    intconfig=""
    sampletemplate="""
    interface f0/0
     ip address ipinfof0/0
    interface f1/0
     ip address ipinfof1/0
    interface f0/1
     ip address ipinfof0/1
```

```
"""
if (routername == "testindia"):
    f0_0="11.0.0.1 255.0.0.0"
    f1_0="10.0.0.1 255.0.0.0"
    sampletemplate=sampletemplate.replace("ipinfof0/0",f0_0)
    sampletemplate=sampletemplate.replace("ipinfof1/0",f1_0)
    sampletemplate=sampletemplate.replace("interface f0/1\n","")
    sampletemplate=sampletemplate.replace("ip address ipinfof0/1\n","")
if (routername == "testusa"):
    f0_0="11.0.0.1 255.0.0.0"
    f0_1="12.0.0.1 255.0.0.0"
    sampletemplate=sampletemplate.replace("ipinfof0/0",f0_0)
    sampletemplate=sampletemplate.replace("ipinfof0/1",f0_1)
    sampletemplate=sampletemplate.replace("interface f1/0\n","")
    sampletemplate=sampletemplate.replace("ip address ipinfof1/0\n","")
if (routername == "testUK"):
    f0_0="11.0.0.2 255.0.0.0"
    f0_1="12.0.0.2 255.0.0.0"
    sampletemplate=sampletemplate.replace("ipinfof0/0",f0_0)
    sampletemplate=sampletemplate.replace("ipinfof0/1",f0_1)
    sampletemplate=sampletemplate.replace("interface f1/0\n","")
    sampletemplate=sampletemplate.replace("ip address ipinfof1/0\n","")
return sampletemplate

#calling this function
myfinaloutput=getipaddressconfig("testUK") #for UK router
myfinaloutput=getipaddressconfig("testindia") #for USA router
myfinaloutput=getipaddressconfig("testusa") #for India router
```

In this case, we define a function that has a standard interface template. The template is now modified with the specific IP addresses and updated depending upon the calling value in the function (which is the router name). Also, we remove the unused lines by replacing them with a none value denoted by two double quotes "" without any spaces between them.

Once we have the generated config, we can use a simple file handling operation to save it:

```
#Suppose our final value is in myfinaloutput and file name is
myrouterconfig.txt
fopen=open("C:\check\myrouterconfig.txt","w")
fopen.write(myfinaloutput)
fopen.close()
```

As we can see, the output for both the generic template and interface configuration can be concatenated or added to a variable named `myfinaloutput`, and that is now being saved in a file called `myrouterconfig.txt` in the `C:\check` folder.

Similarly, we can enhance the script by adding more functions for specific tasks such as **Open Shortest Path First** (OSPF) configs and **Border Gateway Protocol** (BGP) configs, create enhanced and complex configurations based upon specific router names, and store them in separate .txt files that would be ready for the final push to the network devices.

Multi-vendor environments

Sometimes we have many vendors participating in a configuration change or even creating various templates from scratch. We have vendors such as Arista, Cisco (IOS, NXOS), and Juniper that participate in network design in different layers. While dealing with situations such as this we need to be clear which layer each of the vendors is working on and create dynamic templates for each type of vendor involved.

Taking a scenario in which we know the hardware platform and the role of the device (such as access layer, core layer, or **top of rack** (TOR) layer; we can generate configs quickly with very basic parameters.

If a device is in production, we can use the SNMP protocol to fetch information for that device and create dynamic values based upon the return type of devices.

> As a basic idea, we can have a look at https://wiki.opennms.org/wiki/
> Hardware_Inventory_Entity_MIB.
> This has the information on the current open standard **Managed Information Base** (MIB) that is used by SNMP to get basic device information.

Again following good practice, we should ensure we create a generic function that can return the device type. Additionally, SNMP **Object Identifiers** (OIDs) can go deep inside to fetch information such as the current number of interfaces, the state of the interfaces, and even which interfaces are operational so that we can quickly make intelligent decisions based upon a device's current health or information fetched from a device.

We will be installing and using the PySNMP library to query SNMP with device. To install it we will use the earlier method of pip install pysnmp.

> Basic PySNMP documentation can be viewed at the following URL:
> https://pynet.twb-tech.com/blog/snmp/python-snmp-intro.html

As an example, we will try to fetch the current version of a network device:

```
from pysnmp.hlapi import *

errorIndication, errorStatus, errorIndex, varBinds = next(
    getCmd(SnmpEngine(),
            CommunityData('public', mpModel=0),
            UdpTransportTarget(('192.168.255.249', 161)),
            ContextData(),
            ObjectType(ObjectIdentity('SNMPv2-MIB', 'sysDescr', 0)))
)

if errorIndication:
    print(errorIndication)
elif errorStatus:
    print('%s at %s' % (errorStatus.prettyPrint(),
                        errorIndex and varBinds[int(errorIndex) - 1][0] or
'?'))
else:
    for varBind in varBinds:
        print(' = '.join([x.prettyPrint() for x in varBind]))
```

The sample output for the preceding code when queried against a network device is as follows:

On our test router, we enabled SNMP using the `snmp-server community public RO` command, and through executing the preceding Python code written, got the RO string public to read the `sysDescr.0` value, which is in Cisco standards the truncated show version.

Using this method of fetching information using SNMP, we can discover what types of device there are and based on the output, we can make intelligent decisions such as generating device-specific configs without asking for device type inputs.

Additionally, here is an example using PySNMP to fetch the current interfaces on a router:

```python
from pysnmp.entity.rfc3413.oneliner import cmdgen

cmdGen = cmdgen.CommandGenerator()

errorIndication, errorStatus, errorIndex, varBindTable = cmdGen.bulkCmd(
    cmdgen.CommunityData('public'),
    cmdgen.UdpTransportTarget(('192.168.255.249', 161)),
    0,25,
    '1.3.6.1.2.1.2.2.1.2'
)

# Check for errors and print out results
if errorIndication:
    print(errorIndication)
else:
    if errorStatus:
        print('%s at %s' % (
            errorStatus.prettyPrint(),
            errorIndex and varBindTable[-1][int(errorIndex)-1] or '?'
            )
        )
    else:
        for varBindTableRow in varBindTable:
            for name, val in varBindTableRow:
                print('%s = %s' % (name.prettyPrint(), val.prettyPrint()))
```

The output when queried for interface info on our sample router is as follows:

As we can see, we use the `bulkCmd` method, which walks through all the SNMP values and returns the output for the interfaces.

The OID `1.3.6.1.2.1.2.2.1.2` is used as reference to fetch these values from the device.

In a similar way, we can utilize the available SNMP OIDs for different vendors to fetch the specific information from multiple devices and proceed with our expected tasks based upon the returned values.

IP configs/interface parsing

There are many instances in which we need to parse interface configs to fetch useful information. For example, from a list of devices, find all the interfaces that are trunk. Another example could be to find all the interfaces that are `admin-shutdown` (shutdown on the router), or even fetch the IP address configurations from interfaces.

There might be instances wherein we need to find out whether particular IP addresses or subnets are configured on the router.

A good way to extract any information is using regex. Regex is term that is used to match a particular pattern and either fetch the matched pattern or validate whether a certain pattern is present in the parsed text.

Here are the most basic and important regexes that are used in Python:

.	Match any character except newline
^	Match the start of the string
$	Match the end of the string
*	Match 0 or more repetitions
+	Match 1 or more repetitions
?	Match 0 or 1 repetitions
\A	Match only at the start of the string
\b	Match an empty string, only at the beginning or end of a word
\B	Match an empty string, only when it is not at the beginning or end of a word
\d	Match digits (such as [0-9])
\D	Match any non digit (such as [^0-9])
\Z	Match only at the end of a string
\	Escape special characters

[]	Match a set of characters
[a-z]	Match any lowercase ASCII letter
[^]	Match characters NOT in a set
A|B	Match either A or B regular expressions (non-greedy)
\s	Match whitespace characters (such as [\t\n\r\f\v])
\S	Match non whitespace characters (such as [^ \t\n\r\f\v])
\w	Match unicode word characters (such as [a-zA-Z0-9_])
\W	Match any character not a Unicode word character (such as [^a-zA-Z0-9_])

From this string, My IP address is 10.10.10.20 and by subnet mask is 255.255.255.255, we need to get the IP address and subnet mask using regex:

```
import re
mystring='My ip address is 10.10.10.20 and by subnet mask is
255.255.255.255'

if (re.search("ip address",mystring)):
    ipaddregex=re.search("ip address is \d+.\d+.\d+.\d+",mystring)
    ipaddregex=ipaddregex.group(0)
    ipaddress=ipaddregex.replace("ip address is ","")
    print ("IP address is :",ipaddress)

if (re.search("subnet mask",mystring)):
    ipaddregex=re.search("subnet mask is \d+.\d+.\d+.\d+",mystring)
    ipaddregex=ipaddregex.group(0)
    ipaddress=ipaddregex.replace("subnet mask is ","")
    print ("Subnet mask is :",ipaddress)
```

The output when the preceding code is executed is as follows:

```
Python 3.6.1 Shell
File  Edit  Shell  Debug  Options  Window  Help
Python 3.6.1 (v3.6.1:69c0db5, Mar 21 2017, 17:54:52) [MSC v.1900 32 bit (Intel)]
on win32
Type "copyright", "credits" or "license()" for more information.
>>>
==================== RESTART: C:/a1/checkre.py ====================
IP address is : 10.10.10.20
Subnet mask is : 255.255.255.255
>>>
```

As we can see, the regex for the IP address that we used is \d+.\d+.\d+.\d+. The \d means a digit, and + means multiple repetitions, because we are looking for a value of multiple digits separated by three dots.

However, in our case we have this type of repetition in two places, one in the IP address and the other in the subnet mask, so we modify the regex to search for ip address is \d+.\d+.\d+.\d+ for the IP address and subnet mask is \d+.\d+.\d+.\d+ for the subnet mask. The command re.search inside both the if loops returns true if a match is found, and false if a match isn't found. In the example, once we find the pattern in the if condition we use re.search again and extract the value using .group(0), which now contains the matched regex pattern.

Since, we are only concerned with the IP address and the subnet mask, we replace the other string values with a blank or none value so we only get the specific IP address and subnet mask values.

Additionally, using the inbuilt socket library, there might be a reason to check whether the IP address (IPv4 or IPv6) is valid or not. Here is an example of this:

```
import socket

def validateipv4ip(address):
    try:
        socket.inet_aton(address)
        print ("Correct IPv4 IP")
    except socket.error:
        print ("wrong IPv4 IP")

def validateipv6ip(address):
    ### for IPv6 IP address validation
    try:
        socket.inet_pton(socket.AF_INET6,address)
        print ("Correct IPv6 IP")
    except socket.error:
        print ("wrong IPv6 IP")

#correct IPs:
validateipv4ip("2.2.2.1")
validateipv6ip("2001:0db8:85a3:0000:0000:8a2e:0370:7334")


#Wrong IPs:
validateipv4ip("2.2.2.500")
validateipv6ip("2001:0db8:85a3:0000:0000:8a2e")
```

The output for the preceding code is as follows:

```
Python 3.6.1 Shell                                          ─  □  ✕
File  Edit  Shell  Debug  Options  Window  Help
Python 3.6.1 (v3.6.1:69c0db5, Mar 21 2017, 17:54:52) [MSC v.1900 32 bit (Intel)]
 on win32
Type "copyright", "credits" or "license()" for more information.
>>>
==================== RESTART: C:/a1/validateipaddress.py ====================
Correct IPv4 IP
Correct IPv6 IP
wrong IPv4 IP
wrong IPv6 IP
>>>
```

Using the `socket` library, we validate the IPv4 and IPv6 IP addresses.

Another task, as we mentioned earlier, is finding the interfaces that have trunk enabled:

```
import re
sampletext="""
interface fa0/1
switchport mode trunk
no shut

interface fa0/0
no shut

interface fa1/0
switchport mode trunk
no shut

interface fa2/0
shut

interface fa2/1
switchport mode trunk
no shut

interface te3/1
switchport mode trunk
shut
"""

sampletext=sampletext.split("interface")
#check for interfaces that are in trunk mode
for chunk in sampletext:
```

```
if ("mode trunk" in chunk):
    intname=re.search("(fa|te)\d+/\d+",chunk)
    print ("Trunk enabled on "+intname.group(0))
```

The output for the preceding code is given as:

```
Python 3.6.1 Shell                                                    _  □  ✕
File  Edit  Shell  Debug  Options  Window  Help
Python 3.6.1 (v3.6.1:69c0db5, Mar 21 2017, 17:54:52) [MSC v.1900 32 bit (Intel)]
 on win32
Type "copyright", "credits" or "license()" for more information.
>>>
=================== RESTART: C:/a1/checksample.py ===================
Trunk enabled on fa0/1
Trunk enabled on fa1/0
Trunk enabled on fa2/1
Trunk enabled on te3/1
>>>
```

Here, we need to find out the common config that separates each chunk of interface. As we see in every interface configuration, the word `interface` separates the configurations of each interface, so we split out the config in chunks on interface work using the `split` command.

Once we have each chunk, we use the `(fa|te)\d+/\d+` re pattern to get the interface name on any chunk that contains the word `trunk`. The pattern says that any value that starts with `fa` or `te`, is followed by any number of digits with a `\`, and again is followed by any number of digits, will be a match.

Similarly in the same code, we only want to know which interfaces that are configured as `trunk` are in the active state (not shut). Here is the code:

```
import re
sampletext="""
interface fa0/1
switchport mode trunk
no shut

interface fa0/0
no shut

interface fa1/0
switchport mode trunk
no shut
```

```
interface fa2/0
shut

interface fa2/1
switchport mode trunk
no shut

interface te3/1
switchport mode trunk
shut
"""

sampletext=sampletext.split("interface")
#check for interfaces that are in trunk mode
for chunk in sampletext:
    if ("mode trunk" in chunk):
        if ("no shut" in chunk):
            intname=re.search("(fa|te)\d+/\d+",chunk)
            print ("Trunk enabled on "+intname.group(0))
```

The output for the preceding code is as follows:

We added an extra condition to proceed with only those chunks that have no shut in addition to trunk keywords. In this case, we only proceed with chunks that meet both conditions and in the preceding example, te3/1 is not in the list as it is in the shut state.

When validating any IP config, we can parse the config, fetch the IP addresses, validate each IP address (IPv4 or IPv6), and if there are any incorrect values, point out the incorrect values. This can help to ensure we are validating the IP addresses that might have crept in because of any manual copy or paste actions. Of course, this also means we will not see any production issues because the config will already be pre-validated for correctness using this logic.

The code to validate any given IPv4 or IPv6 address from a device config is as follows:

```
import socket
import re

def validateipv4ip(address):
    try:
        socket.inet_aton(address)
    except socket.error:
        print ("wrong IPv4 IP",address)

def validateipv6ip(address):
    ### for IPv6 IP address validation
    try:
        socket.inet_pton(socket.AF_INET6,address)
    except socket.error:
        print ("wrong IPv6 IP", address)

sampletext="""
ip tacacs server 10.10.10.10
int fa0/1
ip address 25.25.25.298 255.255.255.255
no shut
ip name-server 100.100.100.200
int fa0/0
ipv6 address 2001:0db8:85a3:0000:0000:8a2e:0370:7334
ip logging host 90.90.91.92
int te0/2
ipv6 address 2602:306:78c5:6a40:421e:6813:d55:ce7f
no shut
exit

"""

sampletext=sampletext.split("\n")
for line in sampletext:
    if ("ipv6" in line):
        ipaddress=re.search("(([0-9a-fA-F]{1,4}:){7,7}[0-9a-fA-
F]{1,4}|([0-9a-fA-F]{1,4}:){1,7}:|([0-9a-fA-F]{1,4}:){1,6}:[0-9a-fA-
F]{1,4}|([0-9a-fA-F]{1,4}:){1,5}(:[0-9a-fA-F]{1,4}){1,2}|([0-9a-fA-
F]{1,4}:){1,4}(:[0-9a-fA-F]{1,4}){1,3}|([0-9a-fA-F]{1,4}:){1,3}(:[0-9a-fA-
F]{1,4}){1,4}|([0-9a-fA-F]{1,4}:){1,2}(:[0-9a-fA-F]{1,4}){1,5}|[0-9a-fA-
F]{1,4}:((:[0-9a-fA-F]{1,4}){1,6})|:((:[0-9a-fA-
F]{1,4}){1,7}|:)|fe80:(:[0-9a-fA-F]{0,4}){0,4}%[0-9a-zA-
Z]{1,}|::(ffff(:0{1,4}){0,1}:){0,1}((25[0-5]|(2[0-4]|1{0,1}[0-9]){0,1}[0-9]
)\.){3,3}(25[0-5]|(2[0-4]|1{0,1}[0-9]){0,1}[0-9])|([0-9a-fA-
F]{1,4}:){1,4}:((25[0-5]|(2[0-4]|1{0,1}[0-9]){0,1}[0-9])\.){3,3}(25[0-5]|(2
[0-4]|1{0,1}[0-9]){0,1}[0-9]))",line)
```

```
        validateipv6ip(ipaddress.group(0))
    elif(re.search("\d+.\d+.\d+.\d+",line)):
        ipaddress=re.search("\d+.\d+.\d+.\d+",line)
        validateipv4ip(ipaddress.group(0))
```

The output for the preceding code is as follows:

```
Python 3.6.1 Shell                                                    [_][□][✕]
File  Edit  Shell  Debug  Options  Window  Help
Python 3.6.1 (v3.6.1:69c0db5, Mar 21 2017, 17:54:52) [MSC v.1900 32 bit (Intel)] ▲
on win32
Type "copyright", "credits" or "license()" for more information.
>>>
============================ RESTART: C:/a1/parseconfig.py =====================
wrong IPv4 IP 25.25.25.298
>>>
```

We take each line from `sampletext` and find out the IPv4 or IPv6 IPs from each line. Then we parse that information into our IP validation functions, and if there is an incorrect IP, it will print out the IP address that is not correct.

Similarly, we can validate other aspects of the config by creating specific functions and perform a full sanity and validation check on any given config.

Device OS upgrades

Sometimes we need to upgrade devices such as routers, switches, and firewalls. It is easy to perform upgrades on one device, but we need automation to upgrade multiple routers. Different devices have different ways of upgrading IOS or OS images, and the automation or scripts are created with different methods depending on the device.

Taking an example of upgrading a Cisco IOS router; there are two basic steps or tasks that need to be performed:

1. Copy the relevant OS or IOS image into `flash:` or `bootflash:`.
2. Change the config to reload the router with the new image.

Task 1: Prerequisites (to copy relevant OS or IOS image):

- We need a FTP server that's accessible from the router and has the IOS image that we need on the router
- We need the image, the correct MD5 checksum, and the image size for validation

The sample code for task 1 is as follows:

```
from netmiko import ConnectHandler
import time

def pushimage(imagename,cmd,myip,imgsize,md5sum=None):
    uname="cisco"
    passwd="cisco"
    print ("Now working on IP address: ",myip)
    device = ConnectHandler(device_type='cisco_ios', ip=myip,
username=uname, password=passwd)
    outputx=device.send_command("dir | in Directory")
    outputx=outputx.split(" ")
    outputx=outputx[-1]
    outputx=outputx.replace("/","")
    precmds="file prompt quiet"
    postcmds="file prompt"
    xcheck=device.send_config_set(precmds)
    output = device.send_command_timing(cmd)
    flag=True
    devicex = ConnectHandler(device_type='cisco_ios', ip=myip,
username=uname, password=passwd)
    outputx=devicex.send_command("dir")
    print (outputx)
    while (flag):
        time.sleep(30)
        outputx=devicex.send_command("dir | in "+imagename)
        print (outputx)
        if imgsize in outputx:
            print("Image copied with given size. Now validating md5")
            flag=False
        else:
            print (outputx)
        if (flag == False):
            cmd="verify /md5 "+imagename
            outputmd5=devicex.send_command(cmd,delay_factor=50)
        if (md5sum not in outputmd5):
            globalflag=True
            print ("Image copied but Md5 validation failed on ",myip)
        else:
            print ("Image copied and validated on ",myip)
```

```
        devicex.send_config_set(postcmds)
        devicex.disconnect()
        device.disconnect()

ipaddress="192.168.255.249"
imgname="c3745-adventerprisek9-mz.124-15.T14.bin"
imgsize="46509636"
md5sum="a696619869a972ec3a27742d38031b6a"
cmd="copy
ftp://ftpuser:ftpuser@192.168.255.250/c3745-adventerprisek9-mz.124-15.T14.b
in flash:"
pushimage(imgname,cmd,ipaddress,imgsize,md5sum)
```

This code is going to push the IOS image into the router. The `while` loop will continue to monitor the progress of code copying until the specific image size is not met in the directory. The moment we have specified image size, the script will move to the next action, which is validating the MD5 checksum. Once the MD5 checksum is validated, it prints out a final confirmation that the IOS image is not copied and MD5 validated.

We can use this function on any router with just a couple of tweaks to the image name, size, and MD5 checksums for different sets of images.

An important thing to note here is the `file prompt quiet` command. This needs to be executed before we start copying the command, as it suppresses any confirmation prompts in the router. If we get these confirmation prompts, it is tough to deal with all the prompts, thus adding to the complexity of the code.
By adding this command, we suppress the confirmation and once we have the code copied, we enable it to its default state of file prompt.

Task 2: To change the bootvar of the router to a new OS image:

This is where we set the bootvar in Cisco, to point to the new IOS image to be loaded:

```
from netmiko import ConnectHandler
import time

uname="cisco"
passwd="cisco"
device = ConnectHandler(device_type='cisco_ios', ip="192.168.255.249",
username=uname, password=passwd)
output=device.send_command("show run | in boot")
print ("Current config:")
print (output)
cmd="boot system flash:c3745-adventerprisek9-mz.124-15.T14.bin"
device.send_config_set(cmd)
```

```
print ("New config:")
output=device.send_command("show run | in boot")
print (output)
device.send_command("wr mem")
device.disconnect()
```

The output for the preceding code is as follows:

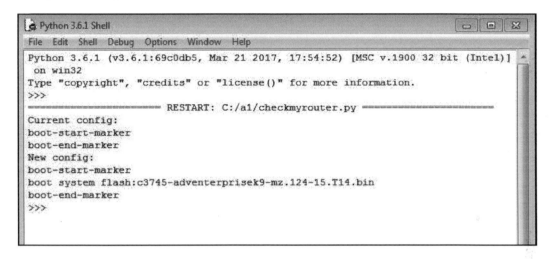

As we can see, in this code we create a command with the new image and send it to the router using the send_config_set method. This method executes the command under config t. Once this is done, we validate from the new output fetched from running the show run | in boot command again, to confirm that the bootvar is now pointing to the new OS image.

If all is good, then we run wr mem to save this new config.

 Once both the tasks are completed, we need to reload the router for the change to take affect. There are multiple scenarios that need to be taken care of before a reload. A direct reload can be performed as Task 3 using the reload command, but as a best practice we need to ensure no production or live traffic is currently on the router, as a reload will disrupt the current traffic flow. Also, it is advisable to be logged into the console to validate the reload progress and for faster recovery if there is a reload failure.

IPv4 to IPv6 conversion

There are multiple ways to convert an IPv4 address to an IPv6 address. In Python 3, we have the inbuilt `ipaddress` module:

```python
import ipaddress

def convertusingipaddress(ipv4address):
    print(ipaddress.IPv6Address('2002::' + ipv4address).compressed)

convertusingipaddress("10.10.10.10")
convertusingipaddress("192.168.100.1")
```

The output for the preceding code is as follows:

```
Python 3.6.1 Shell
File  Edit  Shell  Debug  Options  Window  Help
Python 3.6.1 (v3.6.1:69c0db5, Mar 21 2017, 17:54:52) [MSC v.1900 32 bit (Intel)]
on win32
Type "copyright", "credits" or "license()" for more information.
>>>
================== RESTART: C:/a1/ipv4toipv6.py ==================
2002::a0a:a0a
2002::c0a8:6401
>>>
```

There are many different methods or functions in the `ipaddress` library that we can use for various purposes. The documentation and details can be found at `https://docs.python.org/3/library/ipaddress.html`.

Site rollouts

As we continue to work with multi-vendor environments, there is a demand to quickly roll out devices and configs to get a particular site up and running. Multiple techniques can be deployed for site rollouts, which involves a standard set of devices connected to standard ports with a standard IOS or code image on each device ready to be racked and powered up. To determine the standard **Stock Keeping Unit (SKU)** for a specific site, we can segregate it as t-shirt sizes. At the planning stage we can create t-shirt sizes based upon certain parameters, such as usage, load, and redundancy.

At the lowest level, let's say **extra small size (XS)** can have a single router and a single switch with the router terminating at an internet link. The switch is connected to the FastEthernet 0/1 (for 100 Mbps) or Gi0/1(for 1000 Mbps) port on the router, and end users directly plug in to the switch to get access. Based upon this XS SKU (or t-shirt size), we can determine the hardware vendor, such as Cisco, DLink, or other network device providers, for each of the router and the switch. Next, when we have finalized the hardware providers, we work on generating the config template.

The config template is typically based on two criteria:

- Role of the device
- Hardware vendor

In the same XS size, let's say we have Cisco 3064 (Cisco Nexus running Cisco NXOS) as the router, and an Alcatel switch in the switch layer. As we have now finalized the hardware vendor and the role of each device, we can easily create template configs.

As mentioned earlier, once we have the standard hardware, we also need to ensure the ports are standard (for example, the uplink of switch will be connected from port Gi1/0 to the router's Gi1/1). This will help us by ensuring we create a near-complete template with the interface configuration also being taken into consideration.

A template contains a basic configuration with certain values being determined later on. It is a very generic layout that we can fill in with values from various inputs, such as identifying free IP addresses, the next hostname in the sequence, and which routing needs to be in place as a standard configuration:

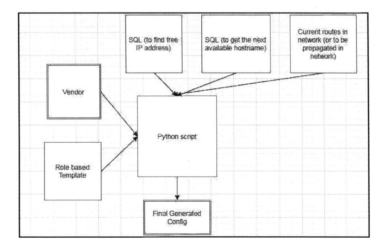

As we see in the preceding figure, the central Python script is calling different functions (with the initial inputs being the vendor and the standard role-based template), and fetching specific information such as free IP addresses, next available hostname (such as `rtr01` or `rtr05`) and routing information (such as **Enhanced Interior Gateway Routing Protocol (EIGRP)** with subnet `10.10.10.0/255` being advertised on the network). Each of these inputs and more (depending upon the requirements) are separate Python functions, with the template being changed depending upon the return values of the Python function.

As an example, we need to get the IP address from a SQL table where the IP address shows as unassigned using Python (we would be using `MySQLdb` library in Python for this):

```
import MySQLdb

def getfreeip():
    # Open database connection
    db = MySQLdb.connect("testserver","user","pwd","networktable" )
    cursor = db.cursor()

    sql = "select top 1 from freeipaddress where isfree='true'"
    try:
        # Execute the SQL command
        cursor.execute(sql)
        # Fetch all the rows in a list of lists.
        results = cursor.fetchall()
        for eachrow in results:
            freeip=eachrow[0]
            return (freeip)
    except:
        print "Error: unable to fetch data"
        return "error in accessing table"
    db.close()


print (getfreeip())
```

This returns a free IP address from the SQL table that we can call into other functions to generate our configs. Of course, once this is given, we also need to update the table to ensure we set the `isfree` value in the record to `false` so that a new call to this function would ensure that we get the next free IP address in the SQL table.

Adding all of this together, we can fetch details from multiple tables and even call APIs for specific tools to get specialized information, and, taking the return values from all of these functions or methods as inputs, the template would be called with these return values replacing the variables specified in the template. Once the template values are filled in, the output will be the final generated config that is ready to be deployed on the router/network devices.

By creating this baseline automation based upon the t-shirt size specifications, the script can be called again with a new t-shirt size that can include a new set of devices, such as load balancers, multiple routers, and each of the different routers in different roles depending on the t-shirt size and complexity.

The next step after the generation of the final config templates is to apply the configs to the router. It is always advisable to perform this functionality using the console. Once we have the basic config in place to get SSH/Telnet access to the device, we can keep a session open with the console while performing the push of the remaining configs on the various devices. Netmiko can be used for this purpose, with the intention of pushing all the configs using the newly generated templates.

Assuming the cables are connected properly, as per the standards, the next step is to validate the traffic and configurations. To do this we again rely on Netmiko to fetch routes, logs, and even specific information such as interface counters and BGP router tables.

Additionally, we could also work on SNMP inputs to validate the current running health of each device. A device can sometime perform well in test conditions, but once production or live traffic is on its data plane, it can spike in hardware resources, causing latency or packet drops. The SNMP stats will give us a clear idea of the health of each device, such as CPU usage, memory usage, and even the current temperature of certain devices and its modules, to display the overall health of the SKU or the t-shirt size site rollout.

Office/DC relocations

There are times when we need to relocate, shut down, or migrate a site to a different location. This involves a lot of pre-checks, pre-validations, and ensuring the same setup of network PoD is active in the other location.

In a multi-vendor environment, and with the increasing SKU size based upon t-shirt size, keeping a track of all active sessions, traffic flows, current interface status, and specific routes manually is difficult. Using Python, we can create an automated way to create a basic checklist and it can be ensured that after relocation the same checklist acts as a post validation checklist.

As an example, we create a basic script that asks if we need to perform a pre-check/post-check and save that in files named pre-check and post-check:

```python
from netmiko import ConnectHandler
import time

def getoutput(cmd):
    uname="cisco"
    passwd="cisco"
    device = ConnectHandler(device_type='cisco_ios', ip="192.168.255.249",
username=uname, password=passwd)
    output=device.send_command(cmd)
    return (output)


checkprepost=input("Do you want a pre or post check [pre|post]: ")
checkprepost=checkprepost.lower()
if ("pre" in checkprepost ):
    fname="precheck.txt"
else:
    fname="postcheck.txt"

file=open(fname,"w")
file.write(getoutput("show ip route"))
file.write("\n")
file.write(getoutput("show clock"))
file.write("\n")
file.write(getoutput("show ip int brief"))
file.write("\n")

print ("File write completed",fname)

file.close()
```

The output for the preceding code is as follows:

```
Python 3.6.1 Shell                                              [ - ][ □ ][ ✕ ]
File  Edit  Shell  Debug  Options  Window  Help
Python 3.6.1 (v3.6.1:69c0db5, Mar 21 2017, 17:54:52) [MSC v.1900 32 bit (Intel)]
 on win32
Type "copyright", "credits" or "license()" for more information.
>>>
==================== RESTART: C:\a1\checkmyrouter.py ====================
Do you want a pre or post check [pre|post]: pre
File write completed precheck.txt
>>>
==================== RESTART: C:\a1\checkmyrouter.py ====================
Do you want a pre or post check [pre|post]: post
File write completed postcheck.txt
>>>
```

Assume that the `precheck.txt` file was taken at the site for multiple devices before the migration or relocation, and `postcheck.txt` was taken at the site after relocation. Now let's write a quick script that compares both files and prints out the difference.

Python has a library called `difflib` to perform this task:

```python
import difflib

file1 = "precheck.txt"
file2 = "postcheck.txt"

diff = difflib.ndiff(open(file1).readlines(),open(file2).readlines())
print (''.join(diff),)
```

The output for the preceding code is as follows:

```
Python 3.6.1 Shell
File  Edit  Shell  Debug  Options  Window  Help
Python 3.6.1 (v3.6.1:69c0db5, Mar 21 2017, 17:54:52) [MSC v.1900 32 bit (Intel)] on win32
Type "copyright", "credits" or "license()" for more information.
>>>
==================== RESTART: C:/al/diffcheck.py ====================
  Codes: C - connected, S - static, R - RIP, M - mobile, B - BGP
         D - EIGRP, EX - EIGRP external, O - OSPF, IA - OSPF inter area
         N1 - OSPF NSSA external type 1, N2 - OSPF NSSA external type 2
         E1 - OSPF external type 1, E2 - OSPF external type 2
         i - IS-IS, su - IS-IS summary, L1 - IS-IS level-1, L2 - IS-IS level-2
         ia - IS-IS inter area, * - candidate default, U - per-user static route
         o - ODR, P - periodic downloaded static route

  Gateway of last resort is not set

       192.168.255.0/30 is subnetted, 1 subnets
  C       192.168.255.248 is directly connected, FastEthernet0/0
- *00:05:31.431 UTC Fri Mar 1 2002
?          ^ -  -
+ *00:05:54.143 UTC Fri Mar 1 2002
?          ^^^

  Interface                IP-Address      OK? Method Status                 Protocol
  FastEthernet0/0          192.168.255.249 YES NVRAM  up                     up
  Serial0/0                unassigned      YES NVRAM  administratively down  down
  FastEthernet0/1          unassigned      YES NVRAM  administratively down  down
  FastEthernet1/0          unassigned      YES NVRAM  administratively down  down

>>>
```

As we can see in `precheck.txt` and `postcheck.txt`, the files are being compared line by line. Anything that is unchanged is displayed as it is, but anything that is different is shown by either a – or +. The – sign at start of the line specifies that the specific line is from first file (which is `precheck.txt` in our case), and a + sign depicts the same line has been output in the new file (which is `postcheck.txt`). Using this method, we can quickly validate the differences between `precheck` and `postcheck` and work on fixing the relevant issues after the migration or relocation.

There are times when we want to automatically run the script to take a backup of the current config of routers. In this case, let's assume that the relocation is planned for tomorrow. Before any activity starts we want to ensure we have a backup of the current device configs.

A simple script stated would do the trick:

```
from netmiko import ConnectHandler

def takebackup(cmd,rname):
    uname="cisco"
    passwd="cisco"
    device = ConnectHandler(device_type='cisco_ios', ip=rname,
```

```
username=uname, password=passwd)
    output=device.send_command(cmd)
    fname=rname+".txt"
    file=open(fname,"w")
    file.write(output)
    file.close()


# assuming we have two routers in network
devices="rtr1,rtr2"
devices=devices.split(",")

for device in devices:
    takebackup("show run",device)
```

The script is going to parse each device in the devices list one by one, execute the `show run` command, and save it in the given filename (the filename is the same as the given device name or IP). However, the next question is how to ensure this runs at the scheduled time. In Linux we have cron job that we can set up for this, and there is also Windows Task Scheduler.

The following example shows the basic process of creating the task in Task Scheduler:

1. Open **Task Scheduler** in Windows:

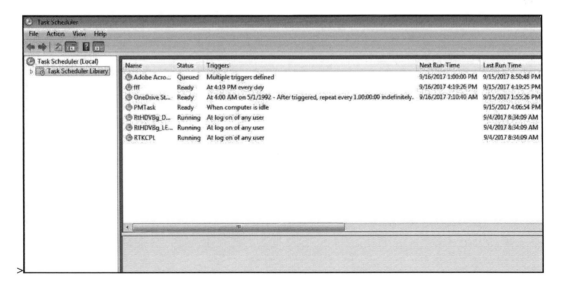

2. Click on **Create a Basic Task** on the right side of the Task Scheduler:

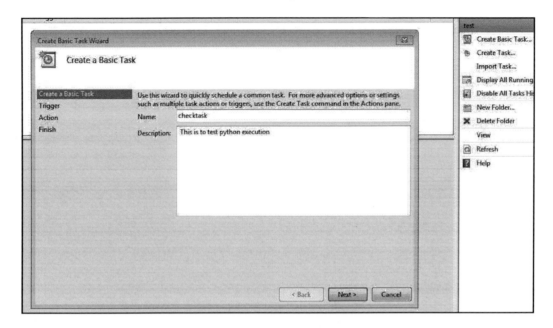

3. Click on **Next** and select the frequency of the task:

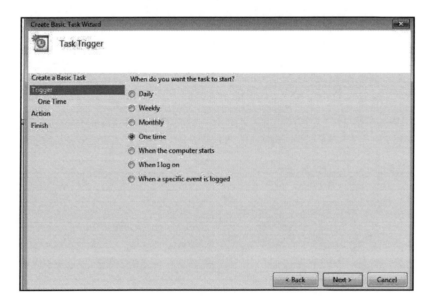

4. Click **Next**, select the time, and again click **Next**. Move to **Start a Program**. At this point, you need to add the details shown in the following screenshot. We have to provide the full path of python.exe in the **Program/script:** window, and in the **Add arguments (optional)** section, the full path of the Python script (with the .py extension) enclosed in double quotes:

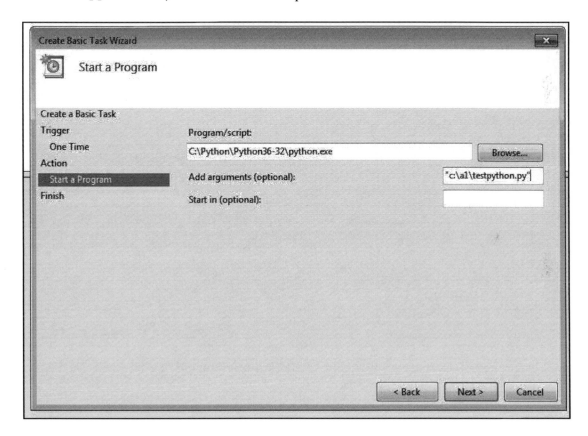

5. On the final page, click on **Finish** to submit the changes and create the task:

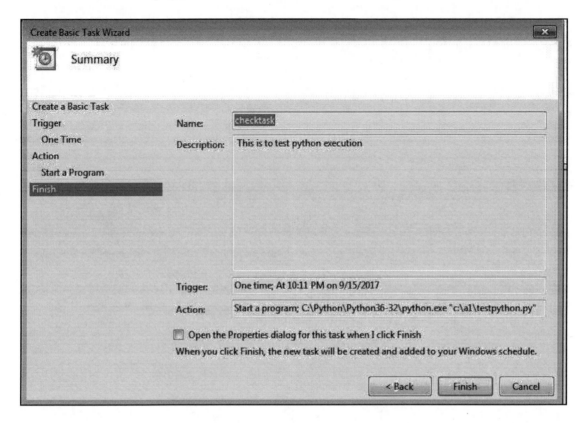

Once this is done, you can run it manually by right-clicking on the created task and clicking on the **Run** option. If the task succeeds, it will return the same in the Task Scheduler window. If all is fine, the task will automatically run at the given time in the Task Scheduler.

This can also be run as a service and at regular intervals, such as daily and hourly, depending on how frequently we want to run the script in our environment.

These scheduled backups can sometimes be taken as baseline and can also act as last known good configuration scenarios.

Bring Your Own Device (BYOD) configs for switches

As our network becomes more scalable, we need to broaden the current architecture designs of our network to incorporate better switches and routers to meet the demand. There may be times when we have a specialized demand and a specific set of hardware needs to be added to our network to meet those demands.

Another requirement may be to lower the cost while increasing the scalability. In this case we would need to add different vendor switches to meet the demand. There might also be a very specific demand for a certain office or a site. In this case, we need to add different vendor hardware to fulfill some specific requirements.

All of the scenarios that we have just observed have one thing in common. To meet demand or specific requirements, we cannot rely on a single vendor solution on the network. There would be a random collection of devices to ensure a particular set of requirements are met. This is where we introduce the term BYOD. BYOD is a new standard that embraces new designs, hardware, and architecture to gel with our current SKU or design. It can be as simple as adding a new mobile phone to our corporate network using wireless, or a bit more complex, such as adding specific vendor hardware to the network.

Architects need to ensure they have good way of forecasting the demand and knowing whether the current network design or hardware can meet those demands. In any case, there needs to be a requirement in the initial design to ensure that cross-vendor platforms are supported with the current technologies. There is a bit of conflict in this design methodology. For example, a certain vendor, such as Cisco, has the neighbor discovery protocol, **Cisco-specific protocol (CDP)**, which discovers the correct Cisco devices as neighbors of the current device. However, to ensure the CDP is discovering and showing the correct information, every device needs to be Cisco. On the other hand we have **Link Layer Discovery Protocol (LLDP)**, which is nearly the same as CDP but is open source, so lot of other vendors including Cisco also have the option to perform discovery using LLDP instead of CDP. Now, Cisco CDP is a Cisco-specific protocol; Cisco has ensured that certain parameters can only be exchanged or discovered using CDP, and for that matter, every device participating in CDP must be a Cisco device.

LLDP, being open source, is limited to parameters that are part of open standards or the **Internet Engineering Task Force (IETF)** framework, and all vendors supporting LLDP only adhere to those open standards for cross-platform and hardware compatibility. This also results in some participating vendors not sending or discovering specialized parameters that are meant specifically for that vendor (such as Cisco). Going back to the earlier point, in this case the architecture design from day one needs to ensure those standards that are multi-vendor or open source only need to be used in a baseline design or architecture. A similar example to LLDP would be using open standards such as OSPF or BGP instead of EIGRP, which is meant only for Cisco devices.

As mentioned earlier, we need to have specific roles defined and hardware or vendor templates that should be created based upon the device or hardware that we are introducing in the current design as a BYOD strategy. Keeping the open standard approach, we need to ensure that the templates being created are generic, and vendor-specific configs can later be introduced into the device.

SNMP is a powerful protocol that helps manage a lot of these cross-vendor or BYOD strategies seamlessly. With a basic configuration of enabling SNMP with a specific read-only community string, we can create quick scripts in Python to get basic information from BYOD devices. Taking an example, let's assume we have two devices that we need to know the type and vendor of:

```python
from pysnmp.hlapi import *

def finddevices(ip):
    errorIndication, errorStatus, errorIndex, varBinds = next(
        getCmd(SnmpEngine(),
                CommunityData('public', mpModel=0),
                UdpTransportTarget((ip, 161)),
                ContextData(),
                ObjectType(ObjectIdentity('SNMPv2-MIB', 'sysDescr', 0)))
    )

    if errorIndication:
        print(errorIndication)
    elif errorStatus:
        print('%s at %s' % (errorStatus.prettyPrint(),
                            errorIndex and varBinds[int(errorIndex) - 1][0]
or '?'))
    else:
        for varBind in varBinds:
            print(' = '.join([x.prettyPrint() for x in varBind]))

ipaddress="192.168.255.248,192.168.255.249"
ipaddress=ipaddress.split(",")
```

```
for ip in ipaddress:
    print (ip)
    finddevices(ip)
    print ("\n")
```

The output for the previous code is as follows:

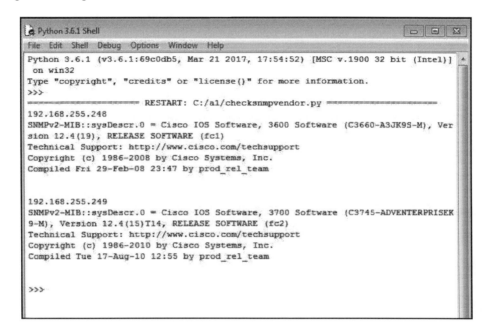

As we can see in the preceding output, now we just need to know the IP address and the open standard SNMP OID, SNMPv2-MIB. `sysDescr` will give the output for both devices. In this case, we can see that one is Cisco 3600 and the other is Cisco 3700. Based upon the information returned, we can proceed with the configuration.

There are various other tasks that need to be performed based upon the BYOD strategy. If there was a mobile phone that you wanted to connect to your network, the only thing needed is a connection to a corporate network and a policy that you could push to the devices to check for various compliance checks such as operating system and anti-virus. Based upon these results, the queried devices can be placed in another VLAN that can be called either a quarantine VLAN, which has very limited access, or a corporate VLAN, which has full access to corporate resources.

In a similar way, as part of the BYOD for switches strategy, we need to perform certain checks to ensure the device is suitable to be part of our network design. Yes, we need to keep an open policy for various types of device, but there needs to be a loosely coupled framework under which devices can qualify to be part of BYOD acceptance.

Let's look at an example that ensures that a device is compatible enough to be part of a BYOD framework. The core requirement is the switch from Cisco and it should have `FastEthernet0/0` as one of the interfaces:

```python
from pysnmp.hlapi import *
from pysnmp.entity.rfc3413.oneliner import cmdgen

cmdGen = cmdgen.CommandGenerator()

def validateinterface(ip):
    errorIndication, errorStatus, errorIndex, varBindTable =
cmdGen.bulkCmd(
        cmdgen.CommunityData('public'),
        cmdgen.UdpTransportTarget((ip, 161)),
        0,25,
        '1.3.6.1.2.1.2.2.1.2',
        '1.3.6.1.2.1.2.2.1.7'
    )
    flag=False
    # Check for errors and print out results
    if errorIndication:
        print(errorIndication)
    else:
        if errorStatus:
            print('%s at %s' % (
                errorStatus.prettyPrint(),
                errorIndex and varBindTable[-1][int(errorIndex)-1] or '?'
                )
            )
        else:
            for varBindTableRow in varBindTable:
                for name, val in varBindTableRow:
                    if ("FastEthernet0/0" in val.prettyPrint()):
                        flag=True
    if (flag):
        return True
    else:
        return False

def finddevice(ip):
    errorIndication, errorStatus, errorIndex, varBinds = next(
        getCmd(SnmpEngine(),
```

```
                    CommunityData('public', mpModel=0),
                    UdpTransportTarget((ip, 161)),
                    ContextData(),
                    ObjectType(ObjectIdentity('SNMPv2-MIB', 'sysDescr', 0)))
    )

    if errorIndication:
        print(errorIndication)
    elif errorStatus:
        print('%s at %s' % (errorStatus.prettyPrint(),
                            errorIndex and varBinds[int(errorIndex) - 1][0]
or '?'))
    else:
        for varBind in varBinds:
            if ("Cisco" in varBind.prettyPrint()):
                return True
    return False

mybyoddevices="192.168.255.249,192.168.255.248"
mybyoddevices=mybyoddevices.split(",")
for ip in mybyoddevices:
    getvendorvalidation=False
    getipvalidation=False
    print ("Validating IP",ip)
    getipvalidation=validateinterface(ip)
    print ("Interface has fastethernet0/0 :",getipvalidation)
    getvendorvalidation=finddevice(ip)
    print ("Device is of vendor Cisco:",getvendorvalidation)
    if getipvalidation and getvendorvalidation:
        print ("Device "+ip+" has passed all validations and eligible for
BYOD")
        print ("\n\n")
    else:
        print ("Device "+ip+" has failed validations and NOT eligible for
BYOD")
        print ("\n\n")
```

The output for the previous code is as follows:

We parse two devices and, using open source SNMP, get the vendor and interface info. Next, we validate, and based upon our conditions we return a True or False. A true condition for all checks results in acceptance of the device as BYOD.

Let's change the rule a bit. Let's say if any device has an Ethernet interface, then it is not eligible for BYOD:

```python
from pysnmp.hlapi import *
from pysnmp.entity.rfc3413.oneliner import cmdgen

cmdGen = cmdgen.CommandGenerator()

def validateinterface(ip):
    errorIndication, errorStatus, errorIndex, varBindTable =
cmdGen.bulkCmd(
        cmdgen.CommunityData('public'),
        cmdgen.UdpTransportTarget((ip, 161)),
        0,25,
        '1.3.6.1.2.1.2.2.1.2',
        '1.3.6.1.2.1.2.2.1.7'
    )
    flag=False
    # Check for errors and print out results
    if errorIndication:
        print(errorIndication)
```

```
        else:
            if errorStatus:
                print('%s at %s' % (
                    errorStatus.prettyPrint(),
                    errorIndex and varBindTable[-1][int(errorIndex)-1] or '?'
                    )
                )
            else:
                for varBindTableRow in varBindTable:
                    for name, val in varBindTableRow:
                        if ((val.prettyPrint()).startswith("Ethernet")):
                            return False
                        if ("FastEthernet0/0" in val.prettyPrint()):
                            flag=True
    if (flag):
        return True
    else:
        return False

def finddevice(ip):
    errorIndication, errorStatus, errorIndex, varBinds = next(
        getCmd(SnmpEngine(),
                CommunityData('public', mpModel=0),
                UdpTransportTarget((ip, 161)),
                ContextData(),
                ObjectType(ObjectIdentity('SNMPv2-MIB', 'sysDescr', 0)))
    )

    if errorIndication:
        print(errorIndication)
    elif errorStatus:
        print('%s at %s' % (errorStatus.prettyPrint(),
                            errorIndex and varBinds[int(errorIndex) - 1][0]
or '?'))
    else:
        for varBind in varBinds:
            if ("Cisco" in varBind.prettyPrint()):
                return True
    return False
mybyoddevices="192.168.255.249,192.168.255.248"
mybyoddevices=mybyoddevices.split(",")
for ip in mybyoddevices:
    getvendorvalidation=False
    getipvalidation=False
    print ("Validating IP",ip)
    getipvalidation=validateinterface(ip)
    print ("Device has No Ethernet only Interface(s) :",getipvalidation)
    getvendorvalidation=finddevice(ip)
```

```
        print ("Device is of vendor Cisco:",getvendorvalidation)
        if getipvalidation and getvendorvalidation:
            print ("Device "+ip+" has passed all validations and eligible for
BYOD")
            print ("\n\n")
        else:
            print ("Device "+ip+" has failed validations and NOT eligible for
BYOD")
            print ("\n\n")
```

The output for the previous code is as follows:

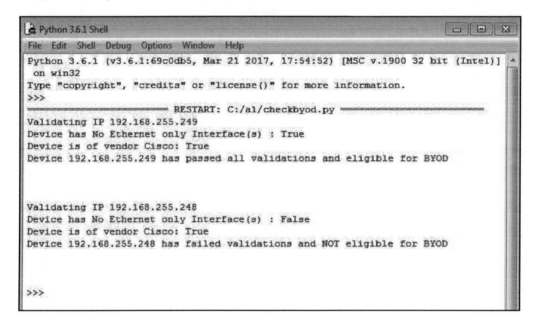

As we can see in this example, we validated for any interface that starts with the `Ethernet` keyword. The `string.startswith("given string")` function is used to evaluate if any given string is at the start of the string that it is being compared with. In our case, the device with the IP `192.168.255.248` had an Ethernet-only interface, which returned the value `True` for validation the Ethernet-only interface. As this is considered a failure for our validation, a `False` was returned, and the script calls it out as a BYOD acceptance failure because this specific condition has failed.

In a similar way, we can validate and ensure multiple checks on on any number of devices, and ensure only those that pass the BYOD framework checks are accepted in the network.

Summary

In this chapter, we looked at various complex scenarios to see how new site migrations and validations are performed. We also looked at the concepts of multi-vendor configurations, creating templates, and generating configs for devices, and also IPv4 to IPv6 migration techniques.

We focused on specialized extraction of particular data, such as an IP addresses, validations of that data, and conditions of failure or acceptance of the data. Additionally, site rollouts and BYOD strategies were discussed, along with best practices such as t-shirt size and validations of BYOD conditions.

In the next chapter, we will go deeper and introduce the web-enabled framework. This will help us create our own APIs and create browser-based Python scripts that can be executed from anywhere.

4

Web Framework for Automation Triggers

As we move on and get better at understanding the coding techniques and Python, the next step is to ensure that scripts are executed without the end users actually running the code locally, and ensure a platform or OS independent approach in code execution. This chapter focuses on putting our scripts on a web platform. We will cover the following topics:

- Creating a web accessible script with examples
- Accessing the script from HTML/dynamic HTML
- Understanding and configuring the environment for the web framework using IIS
- The basics of APIs and creating a sample API using C#
- Using the API in Python
- Creating a task to understand the full end-to-end functionality of a web framework

Why create web-based scripts/frameworks?

A **web framework** is a collection of scripts, hosted on a web platform such as **Internet Information Services** (**IIS**) (on Windows) or Apache (on Linux), and calling the same script using front-end web-based languages such as HTML.

There are times when people ask why we want to migrate our current scripts or create scripts on a web framework. The answer is very simple. A web framework ensures that our scripts are used by multiple end users using just the browser. This gives the programmer the independence to code the script on their preferred platform (such as Windows or Linux), and people can use the scripts on their choice of browser. They don't need to understand how you have written the code, or what you are calling or using in the back-end, and of course, this ensures that you prevent your code from being directly visible to end users.

Let's say you have written a script that calls four or five libraries for specific tasks. There are general libraries, but as we have seen in previous chapters, some specific libraries need to be installed for the tasks. In this case, if you want to ensure that end users can execute your script, they need to install the same libraries on their machines. Also, they need to be running a Python environment on their machines, without which the scripts would not run. So, to run a small script of let's say five lines, users need to customize their environment by installing Python, installing libraries, and so on.

This might not be feasible for a lot of users because of restrictions on their machines (such as installation not being allowed), so even though there is a requirement to run the scripts for those users, they would be unable to use the scripts, which would effectively lower efficiency. But the same users, if given the option, could easily open the browser of their choice and use those scripts like opening any other web page, which would ensure that our scripts bring greater efficiency to the tasks.

Understanding and configuring IIS for web framework

Here we are going to focus on what IIS is and how to configure it, to ensure our Python scripts are executed by harnessing the power of a web server framework.

Understanding IIS

IIS is a tool available on Windows that is used to host web services. In other words, if we install IIS we ensure that the machine on which it is installed is now acting as a web server. IIS is a fully functional program that is available from **Add or Remove Programs** in Windows. It supports the machine becoming a web server, an FTP server, and other things as well.

The following screenshot shows the first screen that appears after IIS is installed and opened using the IIS icon in Windows:

As we can see in the screenshot, the left side of the application indicates the server name, and the right side shows the properties that we can configure for different purposes.

It is important to select **Common Gateway Interface (CGI)** support when installing IIS from the Windows **Add or Remove Programs**. After selecting IIS, Windows gives us the option to select specific sub-items in IIS, from which CGI and CGI support is an option. If this option is not selected during installation, the Python scripts will fail to run from the web server.

Configuring IIS for Python script support

Now, let us configure IIS to ensure it supports execution of Python scripts on the web server itself, and allows end users to directly run Python scripts by calling the web URLs from the web server. The following are the steps to do this:

1. As we expand the properties on the left, we see the **Default Web Site** option. If you right-click on this, there is a section called **Add Application**. Click on it to see the following screenshot:

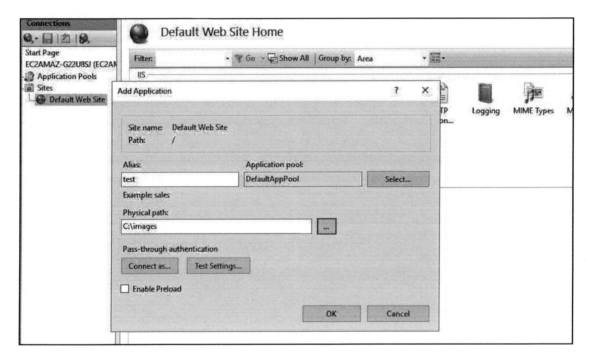

In this screen, we have to enter two specific values:

- **Alias**: This is a value that is part of our web URL. For example, `http://<servername>/test` will be the URL if our selected Alias is `test`.
- **Physical Path**: This is the the actual physical directory mapping on which our scripts will reside. For example, our script, `testscript.py`, has the following path. To call it from the URL we will type the following in our browser:

      http://<server IP>/test/testscript.py

Once we have these values, we click on **OK** and our website reference is created.

2. Now we need to map our Python scripts to use the Python interpreter while being executed. Once we create the website, we see an option called **Handler Mappings** in the right panel. Click on it and open the section as shown in the following screenshot. To add the Python reference, click on `Add Script Map...` as shown on the right-hand side of the screenshot:

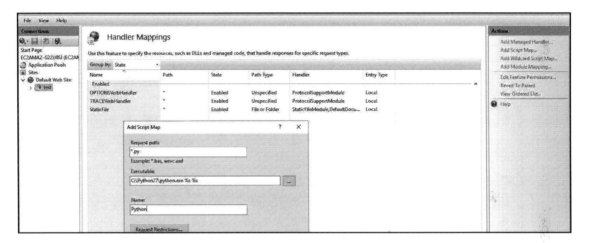

In this section, we fill in three values:

- **Request path**: This is always `*.py`, because any script we call will have the extension `.py`.
- **Executable**: This is an important section where we reference the actual location of `python.exe`. The full path of `python.exe` is needed. In addition to the path, we need to add `%s` twice after the executable file path, because this is interpreted to take arguments passed from IIS. For example, if our path to Python is `C:\Python`, then we would add the following:

  ```
  C:\Python:\python.exe %s %s
  ```

- **Name**: This is simple reference name for the current settings that we have configured. It can be any name of your choice.

3. There is a button called **Request Restrictions** inside the **Add Script Map** section. We need to click on that button, and under **Access**, select the **Execute** option and click **OK**:

4. Once we click **OK**, a prompt comes from IIS to allow the extension. We need to select **Yes** for the settings to be effective:

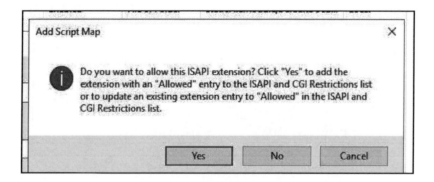

5. As the final step, we select the newly created script map (Python in our case) and click on **Edit Feature Permissions...** on the right-hand side. In the dialog box, select the **Execute** option and click **OK**:

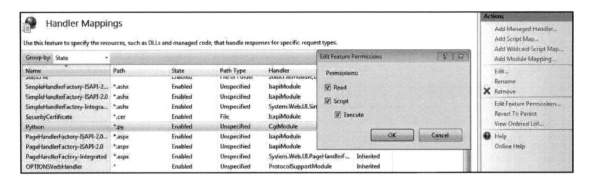

Once all of the preceding steps are followed, we have a running environment that supports the execution of Python scripts from a web browser.

Once the web server is running, you can test to ensure that it is configured correctly by invoking the default page on the web server itself. This is done using the http://localhost URL from the browser, which should show the **Welcome IIS** page. If this does not show up, then we need to go back and validate the web server installation because it means that web server is not up and running.

Creating web-specific scripts

Now that we have a running environment that's ready to run our scripts, let's create a very basic script to take a look at how it works:

```
print('Content-Type: text/plain')
print('')
print('Hello, world!')
```

On IDLE, we type the preceding code and save it as a Python file (such as testscript.py). Now, as we discussed earlier, for our web reference we mapped a physical directory or location in IIS. The newly created testscript.py needs to be in that folder to be accessible from the web.

The output of the web based URL call for Python script is as follows:

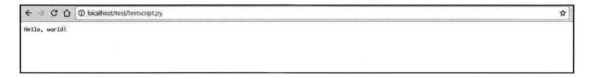

- As we can see in the preceding screenshot, the script is now called from the browser using the localhost URL. The output is a simple `Hello, world !` that was called to be printed in script code.
- Additionally, the value `Content-Type: text/plain` specifies that the return values from Python will be simple text that the browser will interpret as plain text rather than HTML.

Now let's look at an example of modifying it to HTML:

```
print('Content-Type: text/html')
print('')
print("<font color='red'>Hello, <b>world!</b></font>")
```

The output of the URL with modified values is as follows:

As we can see, the first line of the code has been modified to `Content-Type: text/html`. This ensures that the text now being returned from the script is HTML, and hence the last print statement, with `font color` as `red` and `world!` in bold html tag is being interpreted correctly in the browser. In real-life scenarios, if we want to print a pass, fail, or any other specific message or output from our scripts, we should return the values in HTML color-coded and bold formats so that they are clearly readable in the browser.

Let's see an example of printing a table of 5 in a tabular format in HTML:

```
print('Content-Type: text/html')
print('')
value=5
xval=0
tval="<table border='1' style='border-collapse: collapse'><tr><th>Table for
"+str(value)+"</th></tr>"
```

```
for xval in range(1,11):
    mval=value*xval
tval=tval+"<tr><td>"+str(value)+"</td><td>*</td><td>"+str(xval)+"</td><td>=
</td><td><font color='blue'><b>"+str(mval)+"</b></font></td></tr>"

tval=tval+"</table>"

print(tval)
```

The output of the preceding code is as follows:

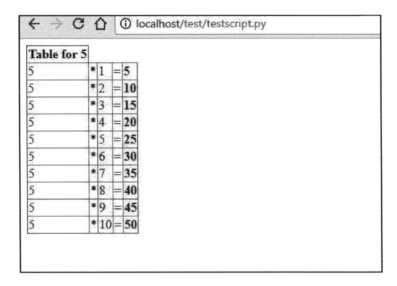

- As we can see, the first line indicates the return type as HTML. In the next few lines, we take a variable named value with a value of 5. Using a for loop, we create the HTML table and its values (for each row and cell) in a tval variable.
- The final statement returns the value of the tval variable to the browser where we called the script.

Getting deeper into this example, now let's create the same table, but the number needs to be provided by the web user in the URL. In other words, rather than sticking to the static value of 5 in our example, the table needs to be generated for the value that is entered by the user in the URL:

```
import cgi

form = cgi.FieldStorage()
value=int(form.getvalue('number'))
```

```
print('Content-Type: text/html')
print('')
xval=0
tval="<table border='1' style='border-collapse: collapse'><tr><th>Table for
"+str(value)+"</th></tr>"
for xval in range(1,11):
    mval=value*xval
tval=tval+"<tr><td>"+str(value)+"</td><td>*</td><td>"+str(xval)+"</td><td>=
</td><td><font color='blue'><b>"+str(mval)+"</b></font></td></tr>"

tval=tval+"</table>"

print(tval)
```

The output of the preceding code is as follows:

← → C ⌂	ⓘ localhost/test/testscript.py?number=8

Table for 8		
8	*1	=8
8	*2	=16
8	*3	=24
8	*4	=32
8	*5	=40
8	*6	=48
8	*7	=56
8	*8	=64
8	*9	=72
8	*10	=80

- As we can see in the change in the URL, we pass the number using the enhanced URL http://localhost/test/testscript.py?number=8. The value specified after the question mark, which is referenced as the value passed to the parameter number, is now taken as an input in the script. The code now imports a specific inbuilt library called cgi to read the parameters passed to itself from the browser.

- These are next two lines:

```
form = cgi.FieldStorage()
value=int(form.getvalue('number'))
```

They are used to take a reference of the form as returned from the browser, and from the form, the specific parameter named `number`. The parameter returned is always in string format, so we need to ensure it is converted to our specific datatype depending on our usage.

- The `value` variable now has the number that we passed from the browser, and the rest of the script is executed in the same manner given in previous examples.

As we can see in the preceding examples, the end user is now only calling the script with specific values based upon their needs, and is not concerned about the back-end logic or program. For the developer, if there is a bug identified in the script, the fix can be done on the main web server as soon as the end users start getting correct results. This also saves a lot of effort compared to users downloading the new fixed script from a specific location on their machines and then running it on their own. Sometimes, even calling the script from the browser with parameters becomes a bit tough. In this case, we use form tags in HTML to pass values to scripts to fetch outputs.

For example, ask the user for their name, the number for which the table needs to be generated, and output the generated table in a friendly manner with the caller's name in the output. Here's the HTML code:

```html
<html>
<form action="testscript.py" method="get">
 Enter your name: <br>
  <input type="text" name="name">
  <br>
  Enter your number:<br>
  <input type="text" name="number">
  <br><br>
  <input type="submit" value="Submit">
</form>
</html>
```

Here's the Python code:

```python
import cgi

form = cgi.FieldStorage()
value=int(form.getvalue('number'))
callername=form.getvalue('name')
```

```
print('Content-Type: text/html')
print('')
xval=0
tval="<h2>Hello <font color='red'>"+callername+"</font><h2><br><h3>Your
requested output is below:</h3>"
tval=tval+"<table border='1' style='border-collapse:
collapse'><tr><th>Table for "+str(value)+"</th></tr>"
for xval in range(1,11):
    mval=value*xval
tval=tval+"<tr><td>"+str(value)+"</td><td>*</td><td>"+str(xval)+"</td><td>=
</td><td><font color='blue'><b>"+str(mval)+"</b></font></td></tr>"

tval=tval+"</table>"

print(tval)
```

The output of the preceding code is as follows:

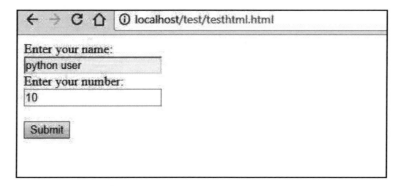

HTML Page

Using the HTML code, we create a form that takes the input needed for our script. In this case, it asks for a name and the number from which the table needs to be generated. Once the user enters this information, the **Submit** button needs to be clicked for the values to be passed to the script:

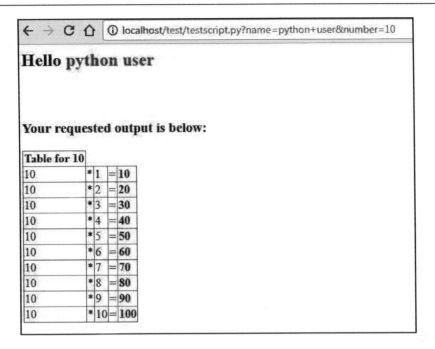

Script Output

As the user clicks on the **Submit** button, the values are passed to the script. In the code, we get the values using the same `form.getvalue()` method for each of the HTML elements. Once the script has the values fetched from the browser, the script logic takes care of what needs to be returned. In our case, as we can see in the example, the username has been displayed in the browser, along with the table that the user wanted to see as the output.

Let's take an example in which we type in the IP address of a device and the command that we want to see from the device, using the form and browser output. Here's the HTML code:

```html
<html>
<form action="getweboutput.py" method="get">
 Enter device IP address: <br>
  <input type="text" name="ipaddress">
  <br>
  Enter command:<br>
  <input type="text" name="cmd">
  <br><br>
  <input type="submit" value="Submit">
</form>
</html>
```

In this code, the only difference is that now we are calling the
`getweboutput.py` script, into which we are sending the parameters of the device IP
address (for the device from which we want the output), and the actual command. Here's
the Python code:

```
import cgi
from netmiko import ConnectHandler
import time

form = cgi.FieldStorage()
ipvalue=form.getvalue('ipaddress')
cmd=form.getvalue('cmd')

def getoutput(cmd):
    global ipvalue
    uname="cisco"
    passwd="cisco"
    device = ConnectHandler(device_type='cisco_ios', ip=ipvalue,
username=uname, password=passwd)
    output=device.send_command(cmd)
    return (output)

print('Content-Type: text/plain')
print('')
print ("Device queried for ",ipvalue)
print ("\nCommand:",cmd)
print ("\nOutput:")
print (getoutput(cmd))
```

The Python code is now taking the input parameter of `ipaddress` for the device IP, and
`cmd` for the actual command that needs to be sent to the router. It again uses Netmiko, as
in Chapter 2, *Python for Network Engineers*, to fetch the information and return it using the
`getoutput()` function:

Sample 1: We provide the IP address and the command show clock:

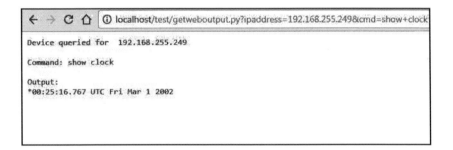

Landing page

Click on the **Submit** button:

Sample 2: For the same script with different parameters provided:

Landing Page

This is the output when the **Submit** button is clicked:

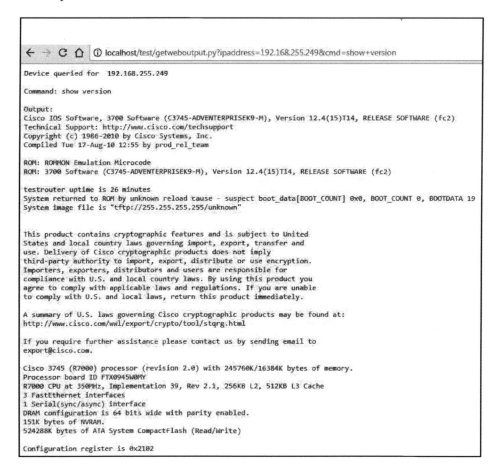

As we saw, we can create a web-based query tool to fetch information from devices with specified commands, which can act as a quick reference for device validations. Additionally, with this methodology we are also hiding our username and password (cisco:cisco in this case) without exposing the device credentials to end users. The end user is only providing inputs on the web page, and is unaware of the code that is being executed at the back-end, which has the device credentials.

We can even have additional checks to ensure that users can only run show commands and display appropriate messages depending on the various commands users will try to call on the web page.

Accessing a script from dynamic HTML

There are times when we run a Python script to create dynamic HTML pages (which are based upon certain triggers that we put in the script). These pages can be enhanced to add additional URLs to invoke other scripts when we click on those pages.

As an example, let's say we need to find out how many models of devices are in our network. For this we create a script, schedule it to run every hour with the task scheduler, and after each run a dynamic HTML page is created to show the updated stats or inventory. In a BYOD scenario, this also plays an important role, because each hour we can monitor what devices are on our network, and if we click on any of the discovered devices, we can get additional information such as a detailed show version.

Here's the Python code to create the dynamic HTML:

```
from pysnmp.hlapi import *

print('Content-Type: text/html')
print('')

def finddevices(ip):
    errorIndication, errorStatus, errorIndex, varBinds = next(
        getCmd(SnmpEngine(),
                CommunityData('public', mpModel=0),
                UdpTransportTarget((ip, 161)),
                ContextData(),
                ObjectType(ObjectIdentity('SNMPv2-MIB', 'sysDescr', 0)))
    )

    if errorIndication:
        print(errorIndication)
    elif errorStatus:
        print('%s at %s' % (errorStatus.prettyPrint(),
                            errorIndex and varBinds[int(errorIndex) - 1][0]
or '?'))
    else:
        for varBind in varBinds:
            xval=(' = '.join([x.prettyPrint() for x in varBind]))
            xval=xval.replace("SNMPv2-MIB::sysDescr.0 = ","")
            xval=xval.split(",")
            return (xval[1])

ipaddress="192.168.255.248,192.168.255.249"
ipaddress=ipaddress.split(",")
tval="<table border='1'><tr><td>IP address</td><td>Model</td></tr>"
for ip in ipaddress:
```

```
version=finddevices(ip)
version=version.strip()
ahref="http://localhost/test/showversion.py?ipaddress="+ip
tval=tval+"<tr><td><a href='"+ahref+"' target='_blank'>"+ip+"</a></td>"
tval=tval+"<td>"+version+"</td></tr>"

tval=tval+"</table>"
print (tval)
```

The output of the preceding code is as follows:

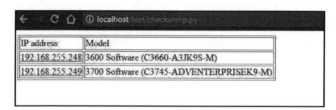

The preceding code creates the dynamic HTML shown in the previous screenshot. It queries the vendor from SNMP for the given IP addresses, and creates the table based upon the values. The blue color in the IP addresses denotes the hyperlink, which, when clicked, will result in the output as shown here:

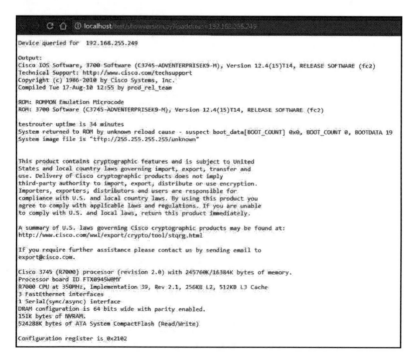

Here's the Python code for the output of show version:

```python
import cgi
from netmiko import ConnectHandler
import time

form = cgi.FieldStorage()
ipvalue=form.getvalue('ipaddress')

def getoutput(cmd):
    global ipvalue
    uname="cisco"
    passwd="cisco"
    device = ConnectHandler(device_type='cisco_ios', ip=ipvalue,
username=uname, password=passwd)
    output=device.send_command(cmd)
    return (output)

print('Content-Type: text/plain')
print('')
print ("Device queried for ",ipvalue)
print ("\nOutput:")
print (getoutput("show version"))
```

As we can see in the URL, when the user clicked on the main dynamic HTML page, it invoked another script (the one that was listed earlier) that takes the input parameter of the IP address from the URL and, using Netmiko, fetches the version of the device.

Similarly, we can gather other stats, such as CPU, memory, a routing summary, and other tasks for each of the devices quickly using the web framework approach.

Creating the backend API in C#

As we move ahead, there are times when as a developer we not only need to consume APIs, but create our own APIs for others to use. Even if we find recurring usage of some functions, keeping in mind web framework strategy, we need to ensure that instead of simply creating functions for that task, we need to convert them to APIs. A big advantage of that is that the usage of our function or task will then not be limited only to Python, but it can be used in any scripting language or web language.

Here we will see a very basic approach to creating a functional API to say Hello World in C#. As a prerequisite, we will need IIS to run the web services, and Visual Studio (Community edition is free to use) to create our own API. Later on, we will see how to consume that API in Python.

Additionally, we will ensure that the return value is in the JSON format, which is the industry standard for API communication, replacing XML.

1. Invoke the C# **Web** project in Visual Studio:

2. Select the **Web API** checkbox in the next screen shown as follows:

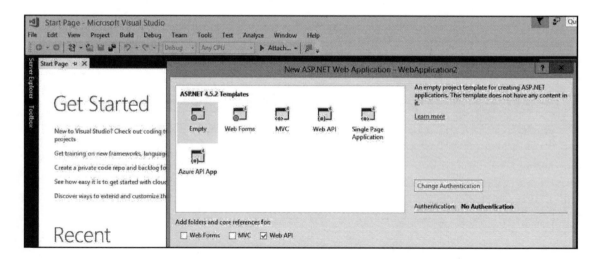

3. Add the **Controller** (this is the main component that will ensure the API framework is active):

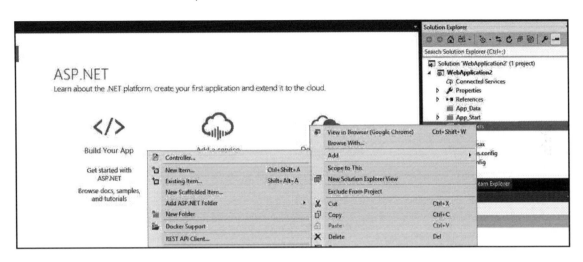

4. Give a meaningful name to the controller. Note, the name must be followed by the word `Controller` (example `testController`), otherwise the controller will not function and the API framework will be broken:

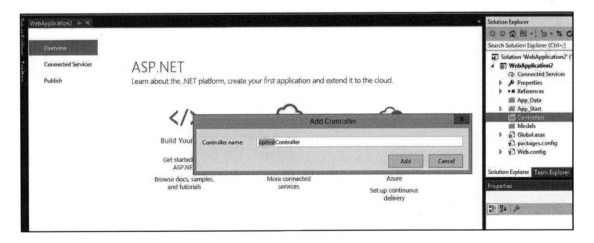

5. Once the controller is added, under the `WebApiConfig.cs` file add the new `JsonMediaTypeFormatter()` config, as shown in the next screenshot. This ensures that every output returned from the API will be in JSON format:

6. In the main `apitestController.cs` program, return the value `Hello World` once the `Get` method is called:

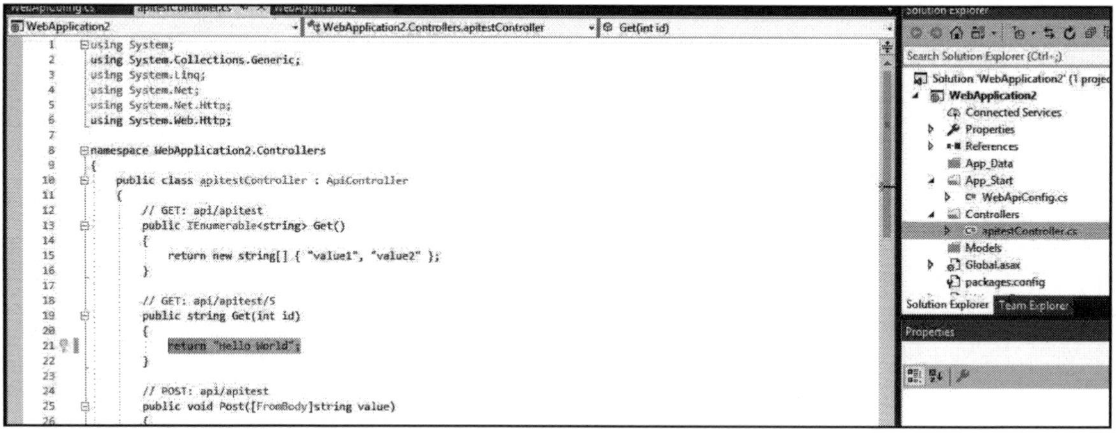

7. Once done, click on the Run button that is available in the Visual Studio application. A screen similar to the following screenshot will be opened, which ensures that the local IIS server is being invoked and the application is initialized for testing:

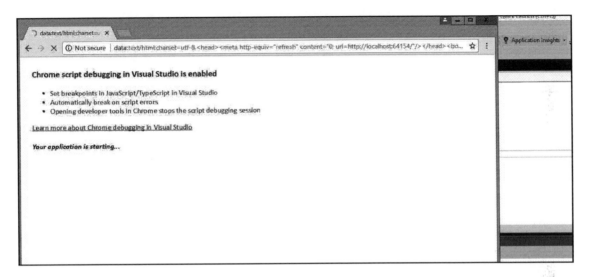

8. Once the application is loaded, a URL similar to the following will confirm our API is working fine. Note that, at this point, the local IIS Express is being used and the API is still not published for external use:

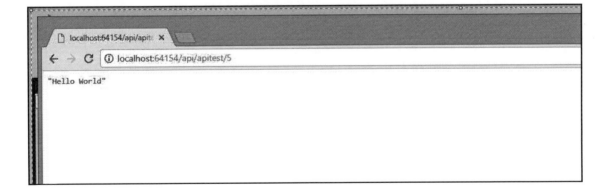

9. Once validated, now we need to publish this to our IIS. Similar to what we did earlier, we create a new application in IIS (named `apitest` in our case):

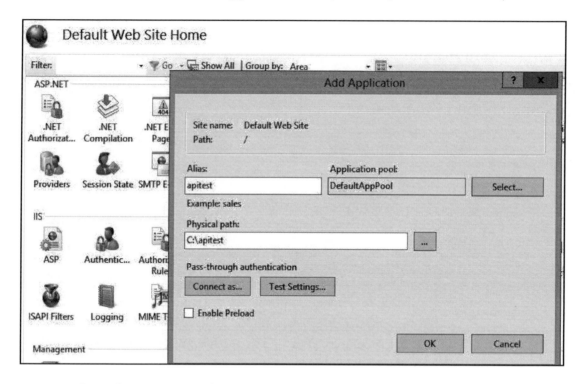

10. Once the IIS mapping has been done, we use Visual Studio to publish our API project to this web folder:

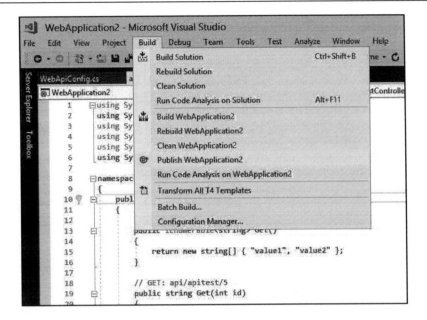

11. We create a web **Publish** profile, and publish it to the local folder that we mapped to our IIS:

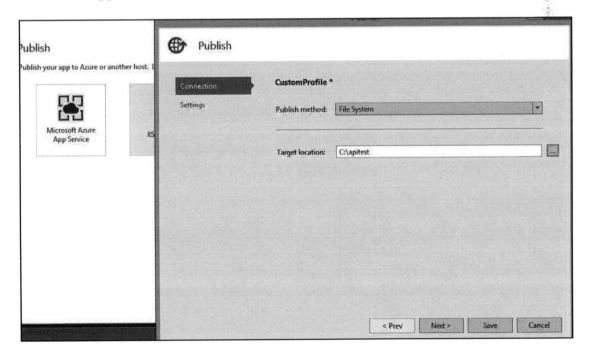

12. Our API is ready to be used. We can validate it by going to `http://localhost` on our browser:

Consuming the API in Python

Now, as we have the API created, let us see how to consume the API in Python.

The code is as follows:

```
import requests
r = requests.get('http://localhost/apitest/api/apitest/5')
print (r.json())
```

The output for the preceding code is as follows:

For API interaction, we use the `requests` library in Python. When we perform a call to the API, the API returns the string in JSON format. The `r.json()` method converts the returned JSON to extract the text value and displays the output as `Hello World`.

In a similar way, we can use the requests library to fetch API results from various web-based API calls. The result is generally in XML or JSON format, with JSON being the preferred return method for the API calls.

Let us see another example to fetch some more JSON from GitHub:

```
import requests
r = requests.get('https://github.com/timeline.json')
jsonvalue=r.json()
print (jsonvalue)
print ("\nNow printing value of message"+"\n")
print (jsonvalue['message']+"\n")
```

The output for the preceding code is as follows:

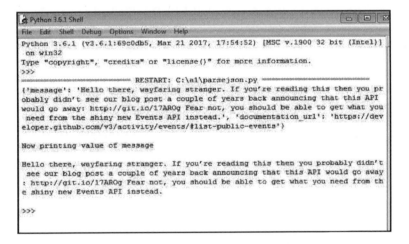

As we now call the GitHub API, we get the JSON value as shown previously. As we can see, the return value is like a dictionary in the JSON return data of the API call, so we can explicitly get the text inside the `message` dictionary key. In the preceding output, the first output is the raw JSON return value, and the next output is the extracted text from the `message` key.

In addition to calling the standard APIs, there are times when we need to pass credentials to the API to fetch information. In other words, there needs to be an authentication in place for the APIs to respond with requested data. In our API, let us now enable basic authentication from IIS:

1. In the IIS, select your website (`apitest` in our case), and under the **Authentication** section, select **Basic Authentication**:

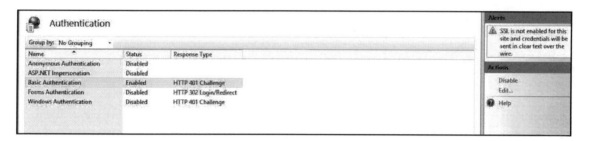

This ensures that any request that calls this API needs to have basic authentication (a username and a password) to access the content. Additionally, we create a simple user `testuser` with a password `testpassword` in the **Users** application on a Windows machine.

2. Since authentication is now enabled, let us see what we get if no credentials are passed:

```
import requests

r = requests.get('http://localhost/apitest/api/apitest/5')
print (r)
```

The output for the preceding code is as follows:

```
Python 3.6.1 Shell
File  Edit  Shell  Debug  Options  Window  Help
Python 3.6.1 (v3.6.1:69c0db5, Mar 21 2017, 17:54:52) [MSC v.1900 3
 on win32
Type "copyright", "credits" or "license()" for more information.
>>>
===================== RESTART: C:\a1\parsejson.py =============
<Response [401]>
>>>
```

We get a **Response [401]**, which means *unauthorized* access in a HTTP call. In other words, the API call is unauthorized and hence no output will be given back.

3. Next, we see the same call, but this time with authentication:

```
import requests
from requests.auth import HTTPBasicAuth
r = requests.get('http://localhost/apitest/api/apitest/5',
auth=('testuser', 'testpassword'))
print (r)
print (r.json())
```

The output for the preceding code is as follows:

```
Python 3.6.1 Shell
File  Edit  Shell  Debug  Options  Window  Help
Python 3.6.1 (v3.6.1:69c0db5, Mar 21 2017, 17:54:52) [MSC v.1900
 on win32
Type "copyright", "credits" or "license()" for more information.
>>>
==================== RESTART: C:\a1\parsejson.py ====================
<Response [200]>
Hello World
>>>
```

In this case, we call the authentication method `HTTPBasicAuth`, and pass the username and password in the `requests.get` call. As we have provided the correct credentials, we get back a **Response [200]**, which is OK in HTTP, and in the last line we print the output of the returned value, which in our case is `Hello World`.

Sample summary task

As we are now familiar with the web framework, let us perform a task that covers all the aspects that we saw earlier:

1. We write a HTML page that asks for the username and password from the user. Those values will be passed into a Python script which will call the API that we created earlier to authenticate. If the return value is authorized, then we display the IP addresses of the devices that we want to view the additional information for on another web page.

2. Next, the user can click on any of the IP addresses to view the `show ip int brief` output. If the authorization fails, the script returns the message **Not Authorized** and will not display the IP addresses. For reference (valid set of username and password):

- **Username:** Abhishek
- **Password:** password

HTML Code is as follows:

```html
<html>
<form action="validatecreds.py" method="post">
 Enter your name: <br>
  <input type="text" name="name">
  <br>
  Enter your password:<br>
  <input type="password" name="password">
  <br><br>
  <input type="submit" value="Submit">
</form>
</html>
```

We have used the POST method in this case, since the password will be shown in clear text on the browser URL if we use the default GET method. In the POST method, there is a separate connection made at the back-end, and the URL does not show the values that are being passed on to the script.

The Python code is as follows:

```python
import cgi, cgitb
import requests
from requests.auth import HTTPBasicAuth

form = cgi.FieldStorage()
uname=form.getvalue('name')
password=form.getvalue('password')

r = requests.get('http://localhost/apitest/api/apitest/5',
auth=(uname, password))

print('Content-Type: text/HTML')
print('')
print ("<h2>Hello "+uname+"</h2>")

htmlform="<form action='showoutput.py' method='post'>"
htmlform=htmlform+"<br><input type='radio' name='ipaddress'
```

```
value='192.168.255.248' /> 192.168.255.248"
htmlform=htmlform+"<br><input type='radio' name='ipaddress'
value='192.168.255.249' /> 192.168.255.249"
htmlform=htmlform+"<br><input type='submit' value='Select
IPaddress' /></form>"

if (r.status_code != 200):
    print ("<h3><font color='red'>Not Authorized.</font> Try
again!!!!</h3>")
else:
    print ("<h3><font color='lime'>Authorized.</font> Please select
from list below:</h3>")
    print (htmlform)
```

3. In case of incorrect credentials (credentials that are not valid, like dummy credentials) being provided:

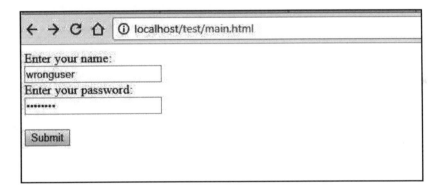

When we click on **Submit** button, it will display the message as shown in the following screenshot:

4. In case of correct credentials (that are correct and authenticated successfully at web server):

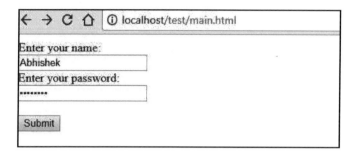

When we click on **Submit** button:

5. Next, we see the IP addresses, which we can now use to get the output. We select the IP address that we want to use and click on **Select IPaddress**:

Once we click on **Submit** (or the **Select IPaddress** button), we get the following output:

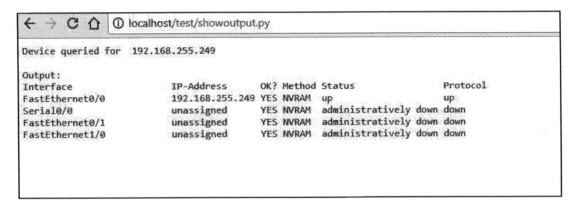

Again, if we look at the preceding output URL, since we used the POST method for this selection, we only see the script but not the parameters that were passed in the URL. This ensures that people need to go from the landing page (in our case, main.html), and cannot directly call any URL with parameters that could have been given if we were using the GET method.

By doing this, we are also ensuring that end users executing this follow a step-by-step selection, and are not jumping from one URL to the other without performing the sequential steps.

In a similar manner, end users can create their own APIs to fetch information such as bulk device names and IP addresses, and can use that information in their script to create front-end, back-end, or web-enabled scenarios quickly accessible from any browser without the need for any end user installations.

Summary

We have now understood the web framework and with relevant examples, the usage of APIs. This includes how to create an API, access APIs, and even work with authentication on APIs. Using this knowledge, we will now be able to develop web based tools for end users. The IIS functionality has also been introduced, which helps developers to customize various web-based settings such as authentications, authorizations, and creating websites.

Additionally, with a fully functional example of a given scenario, readers can quickly build web-based Python scripts, which remove the need for any end user installations of Python and customized libraries. This makes support and bug fixing much easier, owing to having a single machine to fix. A fix done on the server will ensure that all end users will now be using the fixed or enhanced functions of the script, rather than downloading a local copy on their machines to get the fixed or enhanced script.

In the next chapter, we will introduce the use of Ansible, which is a popular open source automation platform.

5

Ansible for Network Automation

In this chapter, we will see the use of a popular network automation tool called **Ansible**. This chapter will guide you through the basics of Ansible, including installation and basic configurations, and will give examples of how to perform tasks related to network automation from Ansible.

This will cover various terminologies and concepts used in Ansible, examples, executions using Ansible, some use cases like using Ansible to create configurations for various devices based upon the templates, and how to fetch some information about the managed nodes from Ansible.

This chapter will introduce readers to:

- Overview and installation of Ansible
- Understanding programming concepts of Ansible
- Playbooks
- Use case scenarios for Ansible

Ansible overview and terminology

Ansible is an automation tool or platform, which is available as open source, and used to configure devices such as routers, switches, and various types of servers. Ansible's primary purpose is to configure three main type of tasks:

- **Configuration management**: This is used to fetch and push configs on various devices that we call as inventory in Ansible. Based upon the type of inventory, Ansible is capable of pushing in bulk specific or full configs.
- **Application deployment**: In server scenarios, many a time we need to bulk deploy some specific applications or patches. Ansible takes care of that as well as bulk uploading patches or applications on the server, installing on them, and even configuring the applications of a particular task. Ansible can also take care of customizing settings based upon the devices in the inventory.
- **Task automation**: This is a feature of Ansible that performs a certain written task on a single device or a group of devices. The tasks can be written and Ansible can be configured to run those tasks once or on a periodic basis.

Another powerful feature of Ansible is IT or infrastructure orchestration. To explain this in detail, let us say we need to code upgrade certain routers or network devices. Ansible can perform sequential steps to isolate the particular router, push code, update code, and then move on to next router based upon the return values of the previous result or task.

Basic requirements of Ansible

Ansible is very easy to install and set up. It works on a controller and managed nodes model. In this model, Ansible is installed on a controller, which is a Linux server, and has access to all the inventory or nodes that we want to manage. As we have seen, Ansible is supported on Linux (there is a beta version out there for the Windows controller but it's not yet fully supported), and it relies on the SSH protocol to communicate with nodes. So, apart from the configuration of the controller, we need to ensure the nodes that are going to be managed are SSH capable.

There is an additional requirement of Python being installed on the managed nodes, since multiple Ansible modules are written in Python and Ansible copies the module locally to the client and executes it from the node itself. In servers running Linux this is already met, however, in network devices such as Cisco IOS, this might not be a possibility as Python is not available on the Cisco node.

To overcome this limitation, there is something called a **raw module** that executes raw commands, like `show version` to fetch the output from the Cisco device. This might not help a lot, but there is another way in which Ansible can be made to run its modules on the server itself, rather than executing those modules on the client (or managed node). This ensures that modules use the resources of the Ansible server (including Python), and they can call the SSH or HTTP APIs of Cisco vendors to perform tasks that are configured locally on the server. Even SNMP can also be used for devices that don't have a good set of APIs (such as Cisco IOS), to perform our tasks.

As we have seen earlier, SNMP can be used in both read and write mode, so using Ansible and running the module locally, we can even configure old IOS devices with the assistance of the SNMP protocol.

Installation of Ansible

An Ansible controller (the main component that manages the nodes), is supported on multiple flavors of Linux, but it cannot be installed on Windows.

For managed nodes, the core requirement is anything with Python 2.6 and above. Additionally, since Ansible uses SSH to communicate with managed nodes, the node must be able to be accessed from SSH. For any file transfers, the default is **SSH File Transfer Protocol (SFTP)**, but there is always an option to use `scp` for the default file transfer protocol. This being said, as mentioned earlier, if Python installation is not possible, then we would be using the raw modules of Ansible running from the server itself.

Going back to controller machine installation, Python 2 (2.6 or above) needs to be installed. In our case, we are using Ubuntu as our OS, hence our focus would be on working with Ansible using Ubuntu as the underlying OS. A way of installing Ansible is to use the **Advanced Packaging Tool (APT)** in Ubuntu. The following commands will configure the **Personal Package Archives (PPA)** and install Ansible.

Here are the basic commands, in the same order they are needed for the installation of Ansible:

```
$ sudo apt-get update
$ sudo apt-get install software-properties-common
$ sudo apt-add-repository ppa:ansible/ansible
$ sudo apt-get update
$ sudo apt-get install ansible
```

In our case Ansible is already installed. Here is a sample output that we get if we run the command `sudo apt-get install ansible` again. In this case if there is a new update available, Ansible will upgrade to the latest version, otherwise it would exit out of the command stating that we already have the newest version as shown in the following screenshot):

```
abhishek@ubuntutest: ~

abhishek@ubuntutest:~$ sudo apt-get install ansible
Reading package lists... Done
Building dependency tree
Reading state information... Done
ansible is already the newest version (2.4.0.0-1ppa~xenial).
0 upgraded, 0 newly installed, 0 to remove and 67 not upgraded.
abhishek@ubuntutest:~$
```

Another way of installing Ansible is by using our well known Python library installation command `pip`. The command for this will be:

```
pip install --user ansible
```

Once the installation is done, here is the information about the folder:

```
abhishek@ubuntutest: /etc/ansible

abhishek@ubuntutest:/etc/ansible$ ls -l
total 32
-rw-r--r-- 1 root root 19366 Sep 19 17:10 ansible.cfg
drwxr-xr-x 2 root root  4096 Oct  4 12:59 group_vars
-rw-r--r-- 1 root root  1131 Oct 12 04:22 hosts
drwxr-xr-x 2 root root  4096 Sep 19 22:42 roles
abhishek@ubuntutest:/etc/ansible$
```

The `hosts` file is the inventory file where we add our managed nodes to be controlled by Ansible. `ansible.cfg` is the actual configuration file used to tweak Ansible parameters. Once the installation is done, we need to add some nodes in the `hosts` file. In our case as a fresh installation, we need to add our localhost (`127.0.0.1`). This node is accessible from SSH with the username `abhishek` and password `abhishek`.

Here is a sample output of our /etc/hosts file:

```
abhishek@ubuntutest:/etc/ansible$ more /etc/ansible/hosts
# This is the default ansible 'hosts' file.
#
# It should live in /etc/ansible/hosts
#
#    - Comments begin with the '#' character
#    - Blank lines are ignored
#    - Groups of hosts are delimited by [header] elements
#    - You can enter hostnames or ip addresses
#    - A hostname/ip can be a member of multiple groups

# Ex 1: Ungrouped hosts, specify before any group headers.

## green.example.com
## blue.example.com
## 192.168.100.1
## 192.168.100.10
##localhost

127.0.0.1 ansible_connection=ssh ansible_user=abhishek ansible_ssh_pass=abhishek

# Ex 2: A collection of hosts belonging to the 'webservers' group

## [webservers]
## alpha.example.org
## beta.example.org
## 192.168.1.100
## 192.168.1.110

# If you have multiple hosts following a pattern you can specify
# them like this:

## www[001:006].example.com

# Ex 3: A collection of database servers in the 'dbservers' group

## [dbservers]
##
## db01.intranet.mydomain.net
## db02.intranet.mydomain.net
## 10.25.1.56
## 10.25.1.57

# Here's another example of host ranges, this time there are no
# leading 0s:

## db-[99:101]-node.example.com

abhishek@ubuntutest:/etc/ansible$
```

 The line 127.0.0.1 ansible_connection=ssh ansible_user=abhishek ansible_ssh_pass=abhishek is where we specify the parameters that are needed to access this system.

We can use any text editor (in our case we are using nano or the vi editor) to add or modify the changes to these files. To modify the `hosts` file, we use the following command:

```
$ sudo nano /etc/ansible/hosts
```

The next step is to verify the accessibility/reachability of the nodes that we added into the `hosts` file, which can be done using the `ansible all -m ping` command as shown in the following screenshot:

```
abhishek@ubuntutest: /etc/ansible

abhishek@ubuntutest:/etc/ansible$ ansible all -m ping
127.0.0.1 | SUCCESS => {
    "changed": false,
    "failed": false,
    "ping": "pong"
}
abhishek@ubuntutest:/etc/ansible$
abhishek@ubuntutest:/etc/ansible$
abhishek@ubuntutest:/etc/ansible$ ansible all -m ping --ask-pass
SSH password:
127.0.0.1 | SUCCESS => {
    "changed": false,
    "failed": false,
    "ping": "pong"
}
abhishek@ubuntutest:/etc/ansible$
```

As we can see in the previous screenshot, the command `ansible all -m ping` pings all the configured nodes in the `hosts` file and responds with a ping. Additionally, in the same output, if we use the command `ansible all -m ping --ask-pass`, this asks for a password to be accessed for that particular node. In our case, we give the password, and then we get the response back. Now, you might ask: *I am performing a simple ping, so what is the need for SSH now in this case?*

Let us add the global DNS server (`4.2.2.2`) in our `hosts` file and then test it as shown in the following screenshot. As mentioned earlier, we invoke the nano editor using `sudo nano /etc/ansible/hosts`:

```
✓ abhishek@ubuntutest:/etc/ansible ☒
  GNU nano 2.5.3                                                    File: /etc/ansible/hosts

# This is the default ansible 'hosts' file.
#
# It should live in /etc/ansible/hosts
#
#   - Comments begin with the '#' character
#   - Blank lines are ignored
#   - Groups of hosts are delimited by [header] elements
#   - You can enter hostnames or ip addresses
#   - A hostname/ip can be a member of multiple groups

# Ex 1: ungrouped hosts, specify before any group headers.

## green.example.com
## blue.example.com
## 192.168.100.1
## 192.168.100.10
##localhost

127.0.0.1 ansible_connection=ssh ansible_user=abhishek ansible_ssh_pass=abhishek
4.2.2.2
# Ex 2: A collection of hosts belonging to the 'webservers' group

## [webservers]
## alpha.example.org
## beta.example.org
## 192.168.1.100
## 192.168.1.110

# If you have multiple hosts following a pattern you can specify
# them like this:

## www[001:006].example.com

# Ex 3: A collection of database servers in the 'dbservers' group

## [dbservers]
##
## db01.intranet.mydomain.net
## db02.intranet.mydomain.net
## 10.25.1.56
## 10.25.1.57

# Here's another example of host ranges, this time there are no
# leading 0s:

## db-[99:101]-node.example.com
```

Once done, we try to perform the same ping test again:

```
abhishek@ubuntutest:/etc/ansible$ sudo nano /etc/ansible/hosts
abhishek@ubuntutest:/etc/ansible$ ansible all -m ping
127.0.0.1 | SUCCESS => {
    "changed": false,
    "failed": false,
    "ping": "pong"
}
4.2.2.2 | UNREACHABLE! => {
    "changed": false,
    "msg": "Failed to connect to the host via ssh: ssh: connect to host 4.2.2.2 port 22: Connection timed out\r\n",
    "unreachable": true
}
abhishek@ubuntutest:/etc/ansible$ ping 4.2.2.2
PING 4.2.2.2 (4.2.2.2) 56(84) bytes of data.
64 bytes from 4.2.2.2: icmp_seq=1 ttl=48 time=10.6 ms
64 bytes from 4.2.2.2: icmp_seq=2 ttl=48 time=10.6 ms
64 bytes from 4.2.2.2: icmp_seq=3 ttl=48 time=10.6 ms
64 bytes from 4.2.2.2: icmp_seq=4 ttl=48 time=10.6 ms
64 bytes from 4.2.2.2: icmp_seq=5 ttl=48 time=10.6 ms
^C
--- 4.2.2.2 ping statistics ---
5 packets transmitted, 5 received, 0% packet loss, time 4007ms
rtt min/avg/max/mdev = 10.603/10.630/10.656/0.094 ms
abhishek@ubuntutest:/etc/ansible$
```

What do we see now? Even though I can easily `ping 4.2.2.2` from my machine, Ansible returns the value of `false`, since Ansible first tries to log in to the device using SSH and then tries to ping the IP. In this case, `4.2.2.2` SSH is not open, and we get a failure message for that specific IP address from Ansible. Additionally, we can group the managed objects under a specific name, such as `routers`, `switches`, `servers`, or whatever name we like in the `hosts` file.

Consider the following example:

We group our current IPs (localhost and `4.2.2.2`) under a new group, `myrouters`. We go back and modify the file `/etc/ansible/hosts` for this:

```
abhishek@ubuntutest: ~
# This is the default ansible 'hosts' file.
#
# It should live in /etc/ansible/hosts
#
#    - Comments begin with the '#' character
#    - Blank lines are ignored
#    - Groups of hosts are delimited by [header] elements
#    - You can enter hostnames or ip addresses
#    - A hostname/ip can be a member of multiple groups

# Ex 1: Ungrouped hosts, specify before any group headers.

## green.example.com
## blue.example.com
## 192.168.100.1
## 192.168.100.10
##localhost

[myrouters]
127.0.0.1 ansible_connection=ssh ansible_user=abhishek ansible_ssh_pass=abhishek
4.2.2.2

# Ex 2: A collection of hosts belonging to the 'webservers' group

## [webservers]
## alpha.example.org
## beta.example.org
## 192.168.1.100
## 192.168.1.110

# If you have multiple hosts following a pattern you can specify
# them like this:
--More--(71%)
```

Notice the addition of the `myrouters` group in the file. Once we save it, let's now use the group to perform a ping task:

```
abhishek@ubuntutest: ~  ⊠
abhishek@ubuntutest:~$ ansible myrouters -m ping
127.0.0.1 | SUCCESS => {
    "changed": false,
    "failed": false,
    "ping": "pong"
}
4.2.2.2 | UNREACHABLE! => {
    "changed": false,
    "msg": "Failed to connect to the host via ssh: ssh: connect to host 4.2.2.2 port 22: Connection timed out\r\n",
    "unreachable": true
}
abhishek@ubuntutest:~$
```

As we see now, instead of pinging all, we just ping the group `myrouters`, which in our case is the loopback IP and `4.2.2.2`.

Of course, results will be the same as earlier, but now we have the added flexibility of ensuring that we perform our tasks based upon either individual nodes or a group of nodes under a specific name.

Introduction to ad hoc commands

Ad hoc commands in Ansible are used to perform tasks or operations that are needed on an ad hoc basis or only once based upon the requirement. In other words, these are tasks that a user wants to be performed on the fly but doesn't want to be saved for later use. A quick example of an use case for Ansible ad hoc commands could be to quickly fetch the version information of the group of managed nodes for some other use as a one time task. As this is a quick information need and does not need to be repeated, we would use an ad hoc task to perform this request.

As we proceed with the chapter, there will be some additional switches (extra options that we pass to Ansible commands), that would be introduced based upon the requirements. Invoking the `ansible` command only will produce all the values that can be passed as options or parameters:

```
abhishek@ubuntutest: ~
abhishek@ubuntutest:~$ ansible
Usage: ansible <host-pattern> [options]

Define and run a single task 'playbook' against a set of hosts

Options:
  -a MODULE_ARGS, --args=MODULE_ARGS
                        module arguments
  --ask-vault-pass      ask for vault password
  -B SECONDS, --background=SECONDS
                        run asynchronously, failing after X seconds
                        (default=N/A)
  -C, --check           don't make any changes; instead, try to predict some
                        of the changes that may occur
  -D, --diff            when changing (small) files and templates, show the
                        differences in those files; works great with --check
  -e EXTRA_VARS, --extra-vars=EXTRA_VARS
                        set additional variables as key=value or YAML/JSON, if
                        filename prepend with @
  -f FORKS, --forks=FORKS
                        specify number of parallel processes to use
                        (default=5)
  -h, --help            show this help message and exit
  -i INVENTORY, --inventory=INVENTORY, --inventory-file=INVENTORY
                        specify inventory host path
                        (default=[[u'/etc/ansible/hosts']]) or comma separated
                        host list. --inventory-file is deprecated
  -l SUBSET, --limit=SUBSET
                        further limit selected hosts to an additional pattern
  --list-hosts          outputs a list of matching hosts; does not execute
                        anything else
  -m MODULE_NAME, --module-name=MODULE_NAME
                        module name to execute (default=command)
  -M MODULE_PATH, --module-path=MODULE_PATH
                        prepend colon-separated path(s) to module library
                        (default=[u'/home/abhishek/.ansible/plugins/modules',
                        u'/usr/share/ansible/plugins/modules'])
  --new-vault-id=NEW_VAULT_ID
                        the new vault identity to use for rekey
  --new-vault-password-file=NEW_VAULT_PASSWORD_FILES
                        new vault password file for rekey
  -o, --one-line        condense output
  -P POLL_INTERVAL, --poll=POLL_INTERVAL
                        set the poll interval if using -B (default=15)
  --syntax-check        perform a syntax check on the playbook, but do not
                        execute it
  -t TREE, --tree=TREE  log output to this directory
```

Some examples of ad-hoc commands are as follows:

1. Let us say we need to ping the same set of devices, but now in parallel (the default is sequential but to make tasks faster, we would use parallelism in our approach):

    ansible myrouters -m ping -f 5

2. If we want use a separate `username` instead of the default configured one:

    ansible myrouters -m ping -f 5 -u <username>

3. If we want to enhance the session (or use sudo or root):

   ```
   ansible myrouters -m ping -f 5 -u username --become -k (-k will
   ask for password)
   ```

   For a separate username, we use the `--become-user switch`.

4. For executing a specific command, we use the `-a` option (Let us say we want to fetch the show version of the routers in myrouters list in a parallel method):

   ```
   ansible myrouters -a "show version" -f 5
   ```

   The 5 is the default value for number of parallel threads, but to change this value again, we can modify it in the Ansible configuration file.

5. Another example is to copy a file from source to destination. Let us say we need to copy a file from the current source to multiple servers that are under, let's say, the servers group:

   ```
   ansible servers -m copy -a "src=/home/user1/myfile.txt
   dest=/tmp/myfile.txt"
   ```

6. We want to start the httpd on the web servers:

   ```
   ansible mywebservers -m service -a "name=httpd state=started"
   ```

   In reverse, if we want to stop the httpd:

   ```
   ansible mywebservers -m service -a "name=httpd state=stopped"
   ```

7. As another important example to look at, let us say we want to run a long running command like show tech-support, but do not want to wait for it in the foreground. We can specify a timeout (600 seconds in our case) for this:

   ```
   ansible servers -B 600 -m -a "show tech-support"
   ```

   This would return a jobid that can be referred later on for the update. Once we have the jobid, we can check the status of that particular jobid using the command given as follows:

   ```
   ansible servers -m async_status -a "jobid"
   ```

8. There is an additional command that provides all the information about a particular node that Ansible can fetch and work upon:

   ```
   ansible localhost -m setup |more
   ```

The output to view the facts on the local machine (localhost) is as follows:

```
abhishek@ubuntutest: ~

abhishek@ubuntutest:~$ ansible localhost -m setup |more
127.0.0.1 | SUCCESS => {
    "ansible_facts": {
        "ansible_all_ipv4_addresses": [
            "172.31.33.197"
        ],
        "ansible_all_ipv6_addresses": [
            "fe80::8a8:51ff:fe0b:6f06"
        ],
        "ansible_apparmor": {
            "status": "enabled"
        },
        "ansible_architecture": "x86_64",
        "ansible_bios_date": "02/16/2017",
        "ansible_bios_version": "4.2.amazon",
        "ansible_cmdline": {
            "BOOT_IMAGE": "/boot/vmlinuz-4.4.0-1035-aws",
            "console": "ttyS0",
            "ro": true,
            "root": "UUID=3e13556e-d28d-407b-bcc6-97160eafebe1"
        },
        "ansible_date_time": {
            "date": "2017-10-10",
            "day": "10",
            "epoch": "1507611083",
            "hour": "04",
            "iso8601": "2017-10-10T04:51:23Z",
            "iso8601_basic": "20171010T045123181202",
            "iso8601_basic_short": "20171010T045123",
            "iso8601_micro": "2017-10-10T04:51:23.181276Z",
            "minute": "51",
            "month": "10",
            "second": "23",
            "time": "04:51:23",
            "tz": "UTC",
            "tz_offset": "+0000",
            "weekday": "Tuesday",
            "weekday_number": "2",
            "weeknumber": "41",
            "year": "2017"
        },
        "ansible_default_ipv4": {
            "address": "172.31.33.197",
            "alias": "eth0",
            "broadcast": "172.31.47.255",
            "gateway": "172.31.32.1",
            "interface": "eth0",
            "macaddress": "0a:a8:51:0b:6f:06",
            "mtu": 9001,
            "netmask": "255.255.240.0",
            "network": "172.31.32.0",
            "type": "ether"
        },
        "ansible_default_ipv6": {},
        "ansible_device_links": {
            "ids": {},
            "labels": {
                "xvda1": [
                    "cloudimg-rootfs"
                ]
            },
```

9. Another ad hoc command that is commonly used is the `shell` command. This is used to control the overall OS, or shell, or root scenarios. Let us see an example to reboot the managed nodes in the `servers` group:

```
ansible servers -m shell -a "reboot"
```

If we want to shut down the same set of servers instead of reboot:

```
ansible servers -m shell -a "shutdown"
```

This way, we can ensure that using the ad hoc task we can quickly perform basic tasks on individual or groups of managed nodes to quickly get results.

Ansible playbooks

Playbooks are simply a set of instructions that we create for Ansible to configure, deploy, and manage the nodes. These act as guidelines, using Ansible to perform a certain set of tasks on individuals or groups. Think of Ansible as your drawing book, playbooks as your colors, and managed nodes as the picture. Taking that example, playbooks ensure what color needs to be added to which part of the picture, and the Ansible framework performs the task of executing the playbook for the managed nodes.

Playbooks are written in a basic text language referred to as **YAML Ain't Markup Language** (**YAML**). Playbooks consist of configurations to perform certain tasks on managed nodes. Additionally, playbooks are used to defined a workflow in which, based upon conditions (like different type of devices or different type of OS), specific tasks can be executed, and validations can be performed based upon the results retrieved from task executions. It also combines multiple tasks (and configuration steps in each task) and can execute those tasks sequentially, or in parallel against selective or all managed nodes.

 Good information about YAML can be referenced here:
https://learn.getgrav.org/advanced/yaml

At a basic level a playbook consists of multiple **plays** in a list. Each play is written to perform certain Ansible tasks (or a collection of commands to be executed) on a certain group of managed nodes (for example myrouters, or servers).

From the Ansible website, here is a sample playbook:

```
- hosts: webservers
  vars:
    http_port: 80
    max_clients: 200
  remote_user: root
  tasks:
  - name: test connection
    ping:
```

In this example, there are certain sections that we need to understand:

1. `hosts`: This lists the group or managed nodes (in this case `webservers`), or individual nodes separated by a space.
2. `vars`: This is the declaration section where we can define variables, similar to how we define them in any other programming language. In this case `http_port: 80` means the value of `80` is assigned to the `http_port` variable.
3. `tasks`: This is the actual declaration section on what task needs to be performed on the group (or managed nodes) that was defined under the - `hosts` section.
4. `name`: This denotes the remark line used to identify a particular task.

Using this example, let us create our playbook to ping our managed nodes in earlier examples:

```
- hosts: myrouters
  vars:
    http_port: 80
    max_clients: 200
  remote_user: root
  tasks:
  - name: test connection
    ping:
```

To create the config, we type:

`nano checkme.yml`

In the editor, we copy and paste the previous code, and save it. For execution , we can use the `--check` parameter. This ensures that on the remote systems, if there is a change intended to be performed in the playbook, it will be simulated locally and not actually executed on the remote systems:

`ansible-playbook checkme.yml --check`

The output for execution of the preceding given command is as follows:

```
✔ abhishek@ubuntutest: ~   ☒
abhishek@ubuntutest:~$ ansible-playbook checkme.yml

PLAY [myrouters] ************************************************************

TASK [Gathering Facts] *****************************************************
ok: [127.0.0.1]

TASK [test connection] *****************************************************
ok: [127.0.0.1]

PLAY RECAP *****************************************************************
127.0.0.1                  : ok=2    changed=0    unreachable=0    failed=0

abhishek@ubuntutest:~$
```

As we see in the preceding output, a simulation of our playbook `checkme.yml` was
performed and the results were displayed in the `PLAY RECAP` section.

Another example is if we want to call specific tasks based upon our initial results. In
Ansible, we use `handlers` to perform that task. In a play, we create a task that can perform
`notify` actions based upon any changes from that task. These actions are triggered after all
the tasks are completed through a handler. In other words, after all the tasks in a play are
completed, only then will the `handlers` condition be triggered (for example, rebooting a
server if all the configuration tasks are completed).

Handlers are simply another type of tasks, but referenced by a globally unique name and
executed only when called by `notify`:

```
- hosts: myrouters
tasks:
  - name: show uptime
    command: echo "this task will show uptime of all hosts"
    notify: "show device uptime"
handlers:
  - name: show variables
    shell: uptime
    listen: "show device uptime"
```

As we can see in the preceding example, the task is executed on `myrouters`, which calls
`notify` to perform a handler task. The `-name` in `handlers` depicts the handler name that
the task will be calling.

> Ansible is case-sensitive (for example: two variables named x and X will be
> different).

---

[159]

Once the notified handler is called, the `shell: uptime` command will run the `uptime` command on the remote shell and fetch the output to be displayed. The `listen` command under a `handlers` section is also an alternate or a more generic way of calling the specific handler. In this case, the `notify` section can call the specific handler under `handlers`, which matches the `listen` declaration with the `notify` declaration (for example, in our case `notify : "show device uptime"` will call the specific handler that is listening to the command `show device uptime`, which in this case is defined by `-name` as show variables), instead of calling the `- name` declaration under `handlers` that we currently see in config.

The Ansible playbook (`showenv.yml` in this case) needs to be invoked with a `-v` switch to see the `verbose` output where verbose output is an output where we can see all the activities as they are happening by execution rather than just displaying only the final result).

- The output without the `-v` command(verbose output is not enabled) is as follows:

```
✔ abhishek@ubuntutest: ~
abhishek@ubuntutest:~$ ansible-playbook showenv.yml

PLAY [myrouters] ***************************************************************

TASK [Gathering Facts] ********************************************************
ok: [127.0.0.1]
fatal: [4.2.2.2]: UNREACHABLE! => {"changed": false, "msg": "Failed to connect to the host via ssh: ssh: connect to host 4

TASK [show environment variables] *********************************************
changed: [127.0.0.1]

RUNNING HANDLER [show variables] **********************************************
changed: [127.0.0.1]
        to retry, use: --limit @/home/abhishek/showenv.retry

PLAY RECAP ********************************************************************
127.0.0.1                  : ok=3    changed=2    unreachable=0    failed=0
4.2.2.2                    : ok=0    changed=0    unreachable=1    failed=0

abhishek@ubuntutest:~$ █
```

- The output with the `-v` command (verbose output is enabled) is as follows:

```
✔ abhishek@ubuntutest: ~
abhishek@ubuntutest:~$ ansible-playbook showenv.yml -v
using /etc/ansible/ansible.cfg as config file

PLAY [myrouters] ***************************************************************

TASK [Gathering Facts] ********************************************************
ok: [127.0.0.1]
fatal: [4.2.2.2]: UNREACHABLE! => {"changed": false, "msg": "Failed to connect to the host via ssh: ssh: connect to host 4.2.2.2 port 22: Connection timed out\r\n",

TASK [show environment variables] *********************************************
changed: [127.0.0.1] => {"changed": true, "cmd": ["echo", "this task will show all enivronment variables"], "delta": "0:00:00.001743", "end": "2017-10-11 04:12:10.20
3", "stderr": "", "stderr_lines": [], "stdout": "this task will show all enivronment variables", "stdout_lines": ["this task will show all enivronment variables"]}

RUNNING HANDLER [show variables] **********************************************
changed: [127.0.0.1] => {"changed": true, "cmd": "uptime", "delta": "0:00:00.002799", "end": "2017-10-11 04:12:10.392302", "failed": false, "rc": 0, "start": "2017-1
04:12:10 up 2 days, 43 min,  2 users,  load average: 0.00, 0.00, 0.00"]}
        to retry, use: --limit @/home/abhishek/showenv.retry

PLAY RECAP ********************************************************************
127.0.0.1                  : ok=3    changed=2    unreachable=0    failed=0
4.2.2.2                    : ok=0    changed=0    unreachable=1    failed=0

abhishek@ubuntutest:~$
```

In the preceding screenshot, notice the output of the `uptime` command in playbook execution (from the preceding screenshot, `changed:  [127.0.0.1] => {"changed":` `true, "cmd": "uptime", "delta":")`. The verbose output states the output and the command that was executed (in this case `uptime`), with the values fetched for the managed nodes.

In many cases, if we have created multiple playbooks and want to run them in a master playbook, we can import the created playbooks:

```
#example
- import_playbook: myroutercheck.yml
- import_playbook: myserver.yml
```

If we explicitly import certain tasks from a `.yml` file:

```
# mytask.yml
---
- name: uptime
  shell: uptime
```

Looking at the configuration inside `main.yml`:

```
tasks:
- import_tasks: mytask.yml
# or
- include_tasks: mytask.yml
```

Similarly, we can call handlers from another `.yml` file:

```
# extrahandler.yml
---
- name: show uptime
  shell: uptime
```

In the configuration of `main.yml`:

```
handlers:
- include_tasks: extrahandler.yml
# or
- import_tasks: extrahandler.yml
```

Additionally when we define variables in Ansible, there are some considerations that we need to keep in mind. Variables cannot have special characters (except underscores) or spaces in between two characters or words and should not start with a number or special character.

For example:

- check_me and check123 are good variables
- check-me, check me, and check.me are invalid variables

In YAML, we can create dictionaries using the colon approach:

```
myname:
    name: checkme
    age: 30
```

To reference or retrieve any values from this dictionary created with the name myname, we would specify command like: myname['name'] or myname.name.

Working with Ansible facts

As we saw earlier, we can gather facts about a managed node using the following command:

```
ansible <hostname> -m setup
```

For example:

```
ansible localhost -m setup
```

Now, as we get the values back (called **facts**), we can refer to those system variables. Each system variable will hold a unique value based upon each of the managed node that was called under the hosts section:

```
- hosts: myrouters
  vars:
      mypath: "{{ base_path }}/etc"
```

The system variables can be called using the {{variable name}}, but in a playbook, they need to be referenced with double quotes.

Let us see an example where we get the value of hostname in our playbook:

```
- hosts: myrouters
  tasks:
   - debug:
       msg: "System {{ inventory_hostname }} has hostname as {{
ansible_nodename }}"
```

The output of the playbook to fetch the hostname:

```
abhishek@ubuntutest: ~

abhishek@ubuntutest:~$ ansible-playbook showsysname.yml

PLAY [myrouters] ***************************************************************

TASK [Gathering Facts] ********************************************************
ok: [127.0.0.1]

TASK [debug] ******************************************************************
ok: [127.0.0.1] => {
    "msg": "System 127.0.0.1 has hostname as ubuntutest"
}

PLAY RECAP ********************************************************************
127.0.0.1                  : ok=2    changed=0    unreachable=0    failed=0

abhishek@ubuntutest:~$
```

As we can see, in the playbook (in the preceding code), we referred to the
`{{inventory_hostname}}` and `{{ansible_nodename}}` variables, which results in the
output in the msg section: System 127.0.0.1 has host hostname as ubuntutest.
Using the same playbook configuration , we can use all or any of the other facts that were
retrieved by replacing the system variables in the configuration.

> If we want to get additional information from inside the facts, we can refer
> to the specific values within square brackets:
> `{{ ansible_eth0.ipv4.address }}` or `{{`
> `ansible_eth0["ipv4"]["address"] }}`.

We can also pass the variable using the command line to the playbook, as in this example:

```
- hosts: "{{hosts}}"
  tasks:
   - debug:
       msg: "Hello {{user}}, System {{ inventory_hostname }} has hostname
as {{ ansible_nodename }}"
```

The execution command to execute the playbook with passing variables:

```
ansible-playbook gethosts.yml --extra-vars "hosts=myrouters user=Abhishek"
```

The output of the command with variables provided during command line execution:

```
abhishek@ubuntutest: ~

abhishek@ubuntutest:~$ ansible-playbook gethosts.yml --extra-vars "hosts=myrouters user=Abhishek"
 [WARNING]: Found variable using reserved name: hosts


PLAY [myrouters] ***************************************************************

TASK [Gathering Facts] ********************************************************
ok: [127.0.0.1]

TASK [debug] ******************************************************************
ok: [127.0.0.1] => {
    "msg": "Hello Abhishek, System 127.0.0.1 has hostname as ubuntutest"
}

PLAY RECAP ********************************************************************
127.0.0.1                   : ok=2    changed=0    unreachable=0    failed=0

abhishek@ubuntutest:~$
```

As we see, the value of `myrouters` was passed to `hosts` and the value of `Abhishek` was passed to the `user` variable. As we see in output of the playbook execution, the `msg` variable output contains the value of the `user` variable and the IP address of the host(s) configured in the `myrouters` group (In this case, the single host is part of this group with the IP address `127.0.0.1`).

Ansible conditions

There are times when we want to execute certain tasks based upon the conditions. `when` statement is used to determine those conditions and execute the specified task if the condition evaluates to true. Let us take an example to execute the `uptime` command, if we pass the parameter clock to the variable clock:

```
- hosts: myrouters
 tasks:
 - shell: uptime
 - debug:
 msg: "This is clock condition"
 when: clock == "clock"

 - debug:
 msg: "This is NOT a clock condition"
 when: clock != "clock"
```

Execution from command line: With and incorrect value `clock123` being passed to `clock` variable):

```
ansible-playbook checkif.yml --extra-vars "clock=clock123"
```

The output of the execution with incorrect values provided:

```
✔ abhishek@ubuntutest: ~  ▣
abhishek@ubuntutest:~$ ansible-playbook checkif.yml --extra-vars "clock=clock123"

PLAY [myrouters] ********************************************************************

TASK [Gathering Facts] *************************************************************
ok: [127.0.0.1]

TASK [command] *********************************************************************
changed: [127.0.0.1]

TASK [debug] **********************************************************************
skipping: [127.0.0.1]

TASK [debug] **********************************************************************
ok: [127.0.0.1] => {
    "msg": "This is NOT a clock condition"
}

PLAY RECAP ************************************************************************
127.0.0.1                  : ok=3    changed=1    unreachable=0    failed=0

abhishek@ubuntutest:~$
```

As we see in preceding output, the message This is NOT a clock condition is
executed based upon the value that we passed. Similarly, if we pass the clock variable
shown as follows:

```
ansible-playbook checkif.yml --extra-vars "clock=clock"
```

The output with correct variable values passed from command line:

```
✔ abhishek@ubuntutest: ~  ▣
abhishek@ubuntutest:~$ ansible-playbook checkif.yml --extra-vars "clock=clock"

PLAY [myrouters] ********************************************************************

TASK [Gathering Facts] *************************************************************
ok: [127.0.0.1]

TASK [command] *********************************************************************
changed: [127.0.0.1]

TASK [debug] **********************************************************************
ok: [127.0.0.1] => {
    "msg": "This is clock condition"
}

TASK [debug] **********************************************************************
skipping: [127.0.0.1]

PLAY RECAP ************************************************************************
127.0.0.1                  : ok=3    changed=1    unreachable=0    failed=0

abhishek@ubuntutest:~$
```

The message `This is clock condition` is now executed based upon the parameter passed. Looking at another example, in a similar way, we can ensure that based upon a certain fact, we can take some action:

```
- hosts: myrouters
  tasks:
    - shell: uptime
    - debug:
        msg: "This is clock condition on Ubuntu"
      when:
        - clock == "clock"
        - ansible_distribution == "Ubuntu"
    - debug:
        msg: "This is clock condition on Red HAT"
      when:
        - clock = "clock"
        - ansible_distribution == "Red Hat"
```

As we see, the condition is triggered on the `ansible_distribution` fact. If the response is Ubuntu, then the first condition is executed, otherwise, based upon Red Hat, the other condition is executed. Additionally, we are also validating if the clock value is `clock`, when the playbook is being called from command line with `clock` as the variable passed to the playbook. In the previous code, both the conditions need to be evaluated to true if we want to get that particular result.

Ansible loops

We can loop for repetitive operations using `with_items`. Let us see an example where we parse the list and print the values:

```
---
- hosts : all
  vars:
  - test: Server
  tasks:
  - debug:
  msg: "{{ test }} {{ item }}"
  with_items: [ 0, 2, 4, 6, 8, 10 ]
```

The output of the playbook execution using the preceding code:

```
✔ abhishek@ubuntutest: ~  ▣
abhishek@ubuntutest:~$ ansible-playbook checkloop.yml

PLAY [all] ***********************************************************************

TASK [Gathering Facts] **********************************************************
ok: [127.0.0.1]

TASK [debug] ********************************************************************
ok: [127.0.0.1] => (item=0) => {
    "item": 0,
    "msg": "Server 0"
}
ok: [127.0.0.1] => (item=2) => {
    "item": 2,
    "msg": "Server 2"
}
ok: [127.0.0.1] => (item=4) => {
    "item": 4,
    "msg": "Server 4"
}
ok: [127.0.0.1] => (item=6) => {
    "item": 6,
    "msg": "Server 6"
}
ok: [127.0.0.1] => (item=8) => {
    "item": 8,
    "msg": "Server 8"
}
ok: [127.0.0.1] => (item=10) => {
    "item": 10,
    "msg": "Server 10"
}

PLAY RECAP **********************************************************************
127.0.0.1                  : ok=2    changed=0    unreachable=0    failed=0

abhishek@ubuntutest:~$
```

As we can see in the preceding screenshot, the iteration prints the value of Server plus the item value in the list for each item in the list. Similarly, for an integer iteration we can perform a loop using the with_sequence command:

```
---
- hosts : all
  vars:
  - test: Server
  tasks:
  - debug:
    msg: "{{ test }} {{ item }}"
    with_sequence: count=10
```

Additionally, let us say we want to print values skipping 2 (even numbers from 0 to 10), the same with_sequence command will be written as:

```
with_sequence: start=0 end=10 stride=2
```

Sometimes, we also need to pick any random value for performing specific task. The following sample code picks a random value from the 4 options available (in our case, `Choice Random 1` till `Choice Random 4`) and displays it using `msg` variable:

```
---
- hosts : all
  vars:
  - test: Server
tasks:
  - debug:
  msg: "{{ test }} {{ item }}"
  with_random_choice:
      - "Choice Random 1"
      - "Choice Random 2"
      - "Choice Random 3"
      - "Choice Random 4"
```

This will pick any random value from the list from the given options under the `with_random_choice` declaration.

Python API with Ansible

Ansible code can be called using Python, using the Ansible API. Ansible has released version 2.0 of its API for better integration with programming languages. One important aspect to note is that Ansible has extended its capability to support development using Python, but it also suggests on its website that, based upon its own discretion, it can also stop supporting the API (creating or even bug fixing its current API version) framework.

Let us see an example of creating a play with the task of seeing the username from our earlier inventory of `myrouters`:

```
#call libraries
import json
from collections import namedtuple
from ansible.parsing.dataloader import DataLoader
from ansible.vars.manager import VariableManager
from ansible.inventory.manager import InventoryManager
from ansible.playbook.play import Play
from ansible.executor.task_queue_manager import TaskQueueManager
from ansible.plugins.callback import CallbackBase

Options = namedtuple('Options', ['connection', 'module_path', 'forks',
'become', 'become_method', 'become_user', 'check', 'diff'])

# initialize objects
```

```
loader = DataLoader()
options = Options(connection='local', module_path='', forks=100,
become=None, become_method=None, become_user=None, check=False,
                 diff=False)
passwords = dict(vault_pass='secret')

# create inventory
inventory = InventoryManager(loader=loader, sources=['/etc/ansible/hosts'])
variable_manager = VariableManager(loader=loader, inventory=inventory)

# create play with task
play_source = dict(
        name = "mypythoncheck",
        hosts = 'myrouters',
        gather_facts = 'no',
        tasks = [
            dict(action=dict(module='shell', args='hostname'),
register='shell_out'),
            dict(action=dict(module='debug',
args=dict(msg='{{shell_out.stdout}}')))
        ]
    )
play = Play().load(play_source, variable_manager=variable_manager,
loader=loader)

# execution
task = None
try:
    task = TaskQueueManager(
            inventory=inventory,
            variable_manager=variable_manager,
            loader=loader,
            options=options,
            passwords=passwords,
            stdout_callback='default'
        )
    result = task.run(play)
finally:
    if task is not None:
        task.cleanup()
```

In the preceding code for displaying the username from managed nodes:

1. `'#call libraries'`: These are used to initialize the available Ansible API libraries. Some of the important ones are:
   - `from ansible.parsing.dataloader import DataLoader`: This is used for loading or parsing a YAML or JSON format file or value if called
   - `from ansible.vars import VariableManager`: This is used for inventory file location
   - `from ansible.inventory.manager import InventoryManager`: This is used for inventory initialization
   - `from ansible.playbook.play import Play`: This is used for configuring a play
   - `from ansible.executor.task_queue_manager import TaskQueueManager`: This is used for actual execution of the configured play

2. `# initialize objects`: This section initializes the various components, such as the root user, `become_user` (if any) and other parameters required to run the play.

3. `# create inventory`: This is where we specify the actual inventory location and initialize it.

4. `# create play with task`: This is where we create the task in a similar way that we create the `.yml` file. In this case, it is to show the hostname for all nodes in the `myrouters` section of the inventory.

5. `# execution`: This is the execution of the play that we created using the `run()` method of the task.

The output of the preceding code is as follows:

```
abhishek@ubuntutest: ~

abhishek@ubuntutest:~$ python checkx.py

PLAY [mypythoncheck] ***************************************************************

TASK [command] ********************************************************************
changed: [127.0.0.1]

TASK [debug] **********************************************************************
ok: [127.0.0.1] => {
    "msg": "ubuntutest"
}
abhishek@ubuntutest:~$
```

As we can see, after invoking the Python file, we got the hostname of the localhost defined under the `myrouters` inventory section in the `hosts` file (`/etc/ansible/hosts`).

Creating network configuration templates

As we are now familiar with the basics of Ansible, let us look at an example in which we generate configs ready to be deployed for some routers. To start with, we need to understand roles in Ansible. **Roles** are used to create a file structure for Ansible playbooks. Based upon roles, we can group similar data. Sharing the roles with others would mean we share the entire defined file structure for a common set of content. A typical role file structure would contain the main folder and the content folder, and under the content folder, we would have `templates`, `vars`, and `tasks` folders.

In our case, the hierarchy is as follows:

- Main directory
    - -Roles
        - -Routers
            - -Templates
            - -Vars
            - -Tasks

Under each of the templates, vars, or tasks folders, if we call that specific role, a file named `main.yml` is searched automatically and any configs in that file are taken into consideration for that particular role. Using the details of hierarchy as previously mentioned , in our test machine (running Ubuntu) here is how our file structure looks in the example:

```
✔ abhishek@ubuntutest: ~/rtrconfig  ☒
abhishek@ubuntutest:~/rtrconfig$ find . -type d
.
./roles
./roles/routers
./roles/routers/templates
./roles/routers/vars
./roles/routers/tasks
abhishek@ubuntutest:~/rtrconfig$
```

As we see, under the `rtrconfig` folder, we have defined the folders as per Ansible standards. Once we create the folder hierarchy, the next step is to configure/create the files under each of the sections, based upon our requirements.

To start with, as we will be using a router template to generate the configs, we create a template and put it in the `roles/routers/templates` folder.

Router config template is as follows (used as a generic router template to generate router configs):

```
no service pad
 service tcp-keepalives-in
 service tcp-keepalives-out
 service password-encryption
 username test password test
 !
 hostname {{item.hostname}}
 logging server {{logging_server}}
 !
 logging buffered 32000
 no logging console
 !
 ip domain-lookup enable
 !
 exit
```

As we can see in the template, `{{item.hostname}}` and `{{logging_server}}` are two values that we would replace while creating the actual config. As this is a Jinja template, we would save this template as `somename.j2` (in our case, `routers.j2`). The next step is to define the variable values.

As we saw earlier, we need to ensure that the `logging_server` variable has already been defined a value. This will be in the `roles/routers/vars` folder:

```
---
logging_server: 10.10.10.10
```

We save this file as `main.yml` in the `vars` folder, which will be picked by default while executing the playbook for the variable value declarations. Once we have the definitions and template in place, the next step is to define the actual task that needs to be performed.

This will be done in the `roles/routers/tasks` folder and again saved as `main.yml` for auto discovery during the execution of that specific role.

Let us see the config for this:

```
---
- name: Generate configuration files
  template: src=routers.j2 dest=/home/abhishek/{{item.hostname}}.txt
  with_items:
  - { hostname: myrouter1 }
  - { hostname: myrouter2 }
```

In the config for the task, we call the template that we created (in this case, `routers.j2`), and provide a destination folder where the config files will be saved (in this case, `/home/abhishek/{{item.hostname}}.txt`).

A specific point to note here is that `{{item.hostname}}` will resolve to each of the hostnames that we have provided using the `with_items` loop. As a result, the filename that will be generated will be each item defined in the `with_items` loop (in our case, `myrouter1.txt` and `myrouter2.txt`).

As mentioned previously, the `with_items` will loop with each value, with the hostname variable value being changed with each iteration. Once we have the template, vars, and task created, we will call the role in our main playbook and get it executed.

The main playbook config is as follows:

```
---
- name: Generate router configuration files
  hosts: localhost

  roles:
    - routers
```

Here we just call the hosts (which is localhost in our case since we want to get this executed locally), and call the role that needs to be executed in the playbook (in our case, `routers`). We save it as any name with a `.yml` extension (in our case, `makeconfig.yml`).

The final validation to ensure all `.yml` files are created in respective folders are as follows:

1. To recap, here is the detailed file structure, as we now see the files under the `rtrconfig` folder:

```
abhishek@ubuntutest: ~/rtrconfig  ✖
abhishek@ubuntutest:~/rtrconfig$ find .
.
./makeconfig.yml
./roles
./roles/routers
./roles/routers/templates
./roles/routers/templates/routers.j2
./roles/routers/vars
./roles/routers/vars/main.yml
./roles/routers/tasks
./roles/routers/tasks/main.yml
abhishek@ubuntutest:~/rtrconfig$
```

2. To generate the config for routers , we execute the `makeconfig.yml` playbook:

```
abhishek@ubuntutest: ~/rtrconfig  ✖
abhishek@ubuntutest:~/rtrconfig$ ansible-playbook makeconfig.yml

PLAY [Generate router configuration files] *************************************

TASK [Gathering Facts] ********************************************************
ok: [127.0.0.1]

TASK [routers : Generate configuration files] *********************************
changed: [127.0.0.1] => (item={u'hostname': u'myrouter1'})
changed: [127.0.0.1] => (item={u'hostname': u'myrouter2'})

PLAY RECAP ********************************************************************
127.0.0.1                  : ok=2    changed=1    unreachable=0    failed=0

abhishek@ubuntutest:~/rtrconfig$
```

3. Once executed successfully, we should have two files (`myrouter1.txt` and `myrouter2.txt`) in the `/home/abhishek` folder with the generated config:

```
abhishek@ubuntutest: ~    ☒
abhishek@ubuntutest:~$ ls -l my*.txt
-rw-r--r-- 1 abhishek root 250 Oct 24 04:36 myrouter1.txt
-rw-r--r-- 1 abhishek root 250 Oct 24 04:36 myrouter2.txt
abhishek@ubuntutest:~$
```

4. Here is the content from one of the generated files:

```
abhishek@ubuntutest: ~    ☒
abhishek@ubuntutest:~$ more myrouter1.txt
no service pad
service tcp-keepalives-in
service tcp-keepalives-out
service password-encryption
username test password test
!
hostname myrouter1
logging server 10.10.10.10
!
logging buffered 32000
no logging console
!
ip domain-lookup enable
!
exit

abhishek@ubuntutest:~$
```

5. As we can see, now we have a generated config, using the template, with the values replaced for the hostname and `logging _server` section.

The config is now generated and ready to be pushed on those particular routers (which were part of `main.yml` under `roles/routers/tasks`), and in a similar way, we can generate configs with various roles and multiple devices in each role, such as switches, routers, load balancers, and so on with each role containing specific information, such as variables, templates, and tasks relevant to that role.

Summary

In this chapter, we learned what Ansible is, its installation, and basic usage of Ansible. This chapter also introduced concepts and terminology used in Ansible, with reference to how to create playbooks, tasks, and other basic functions in Ansible. We also got familar with ad-hoc commands and understand the concept of facts and their usage in Ansible.

Finally, using Jinja templates we understood how to create a full configuration using templates with reference to device/role specific information using roles in Ansible.

In the next chapter, we will see how to call miscellaneous other aspects of automation, such as using Splunk for syslog collection and fetching information from Python, working with basic automation on BGP, UC integration examples, and other relevant examples that can be used for ready reference when creating automation scripts.

6

Continuous Integration for Network Engineers

As we saw in previous chapters, now armed with knowledge or a fair understanding on creating automation using various techniques, working with Ansible, and understanding best practices, we continue our journey to understand how to work on the basics of planning an automation project.

In this chapter, we will see some of the tools that help us in working on planning our automation projects, and some examples to interact with some increasingly complex scenarios related to various devices or network technologies.

Some of the aspects that we will be working on are:

- Interaction with Splunk
- BGP and routing table
- Wireless client to AP to switchport
- Phone to switchport
- WLAN and IPAM
- Useful best practices and use cases

Interaction with Splunk

Splunk is one of the most widely used data mining tools. With its data mining and digging capabilities, engineers can take actions based upon decisions. While it is useful in various aspects, here we will see an example of Splunk being used as a Syslog server, with our test router sending a message (as syslog) to this server, and how from automation we can query results from Splunk for these syslogs and take actions.

This is an important part of automation, since based upon certain events (alerts and syslogs), engineers need to perform automated tasks, like self healing, or even triggering emails or using third-party tools to create tickets for various teams to work on.

Here we will see the basic implementation and configuration of Splunk as a Syslog server:

1. After downloading and installing Splunk , it can be accessed from the URL `http://localhost:8000/en-US/account/login?return_to=%2Fen-US%2F` as we can see in the following screenshot:

2. Once we login, we create a listener listed to syslogs (in our case we use the TCP protocol and keep the default port 514 open):

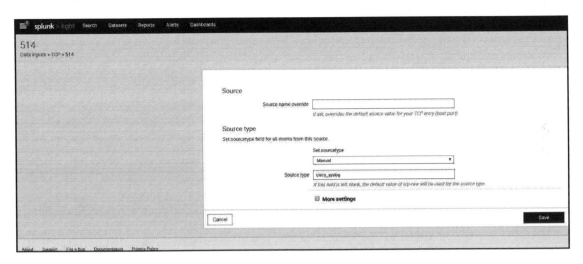

Once the configuration is done for TCP port 514 on Splunk (listening for syslog messages), ensure any local firewall on the server is allowing inbound packets to TCP port 514, and our machine is ready to access syslogs from network devices on TCP port 514).

3. Configure the router to send syslogs. We apply the following commands on the router to enable logging (In our case the IP for the Syslog server is 192.168.255.250):

```
config t
logging host 192.168.255.250 transport tcp port 514
logging buffered informational
exit
```

This configures the router to send syslogs to the given IP address on TCP protocol over port 514. Additionally, we are also stating to log only information syslog messages on the router.

4. Once done, for confirmation we can try to perform a shutdown and no shutdown of any interface (`Loopback0` in our case), and see the log using the `show logging` command on the router:

```
R2#show logging
Syslog logging: enabled (11 messages dropped, 0 messages rate-
limited,
                   0 flushes, 0 overruns, xml disabled, filtering
disabled)
    Console logging: level debugging, 26 messages logged, xml
disabled,
                     filtering disabled
    Monitor logging: level debugging, 0 messages logged, xml
disabled,
                     filtering disabled
    Buffer logging: level informational, 7 messages logged, xml
disabled,
                     filtering disabled
    Logging Exception size (4096 bytes)
    Count and timestamp logging messages: disabled
No active filter modules.
    Trap logging: level informational, 30 message lines logged
         Logging to 192.168.255.250(global) (tcp port 514, audit
disabled, link up), 30 message lines logged, xml disabled,
                     filtering disabled
Log Buffer (4096 bytes):
*Mar  1 01:02:04.223: %SYS-5-CONFIG_I: Configured from console
by console
*Mar  1 01:02:10.275: %SYS-6-LOGGINGHOST_STARTSTOP: Logging to
host 192.168.255.250 started - reconnection
*Mar  1 01:02:32.179: %LINK-5-CHANGED: Interface Loopback0,
changed state to administratively down
*Mar  1 01:02:33.179: %LINEPROTO-5-UPDOWN: Line protocol on
Interface Loopback0, changed state to down
*Mar  1 01:02:39.303: %SYS-5-CONFIG_I: Configured from console
by console
*Mar  1 01:02:39.647: %LINK-3-UPDOWN: Interface Loopback0,
changed state to up
*Mar  1 01:02:40.647: %LINEPROTO-5-UPDOWN: Line protocol on
Interface Loopback0, changed state to up
```

An important aspect to confirm if the router is sending syslogs is the line `tcp port 514, audit disabled, link up,` which confirms that the router is sending syslog traffic to the Syslog server.

5. Here is the raw output on Splunk for the syslog that is generated:

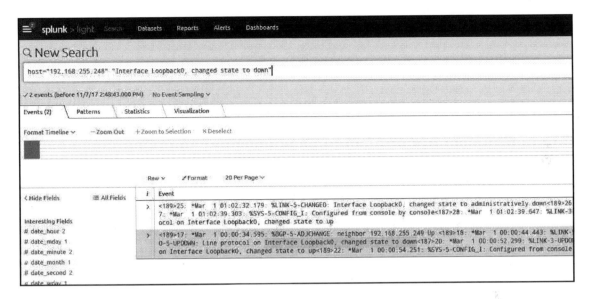

As we see in the **New Search** section we can write queries to fetch the exact data that we want. In our case we wanted to see only the log from our router with the Interface Loopback0 down messages, hence we wrote the query:

```
host="192.168.255.248" "Interface Loopback0, changed state to
down"
```

6. Now let us see the code from Python that we can write to fetch the same information using a script:

```python
import requests
import json
from xml.dom import minidom

username="admin"
password="admin"

### For generating the session key ####
url = 'https://localhost:8089/services/auth/login'
headers = {'Content-Type': 'application/json'}
data={"username":username,"password":password}
requests.packages.urllib3.disable_warnings()
r = requests.get(url, auth=(username, password), data=data,
headers=headers,verify=False)
sessionkey =
```

```
minidom.parseString(r.text).getElementsByTagName('sessionKey')[
0].childNodes[0].nodeValue

#### For executing the query using the generated sessionkey
headers={"Authorization":"Splunk "+sessionkey}
data={"search":'search host="192.168.255.248" "Interface
Loopback0, changed state to down"','output_mode':"json"}
r=requests.post('https://localhost:8089/servicesNS/admin/search
/search/jobs/export',data=data , headers=headers,verify=False);
print (r.text)
```

In the first section, we query the API of Splunk to fetch the authentication session key (or token) to run our queries and get results. Once we have the session key (extracted from the XML output), we create a header and using `requests.post` we execute our query. The data variable contains our query in the following format:

```
{"search":'search host="192.168.255.248" "Interface Loopback0,
changed state to down"'}
```

In other words, if we take this in a variable (named `Search`), and provide the result as a value to that variable, it would look like below:

```
Search='search host="192.168.255.248" "Interface Loopback0,
changed state to down"'
```

Additionally we also send another option of `output_mode` as JSON , since we want the output in JSON (some other values can be CSV or XML).

Executing the same will get the following output:

As we see in the preceding output, we are now retrieving and displaying the value in JSON format.

We will stop our example here, but to enhance this script, this result can now become a trigger on which we can add additional methods or logic to decide on the trigger for further actions. By this logic, we can have self-healing scripts that find out the data (as a trigger), evaluate the trigger (identify it actionable), and take actions based upon further logic.

Automation examples on various technology domains

With the familiarity and understanding of automation with the interaction of devices, APIs, controllers, let's see some examples of how to interact with other network domain devices and tackle some complex scenarios using automation frameworks.

Some of these examples will be a small project in themselves, but will help you understand additional ways of performing automation tasks in depth.

BGP and routing table

Let's take an example in which we need to configure BGP, validate if a session is up, and report the details for the same. In our example, we would take two routers (as a prerequisite, both routers are able to ping each other) as follows:

As we see R2 and testrouter are able to ping each other using an IP address of the FastEthernet0/0 interface of each other.

The next step is a very basic configuration of BGP (in our case, we use the **Autonomous System (AS)** number 200). The code is as follows:

```
from netmiko import ConnectHandler
import time

def pushbgpconfig(routerip,remoteip,localas,remoteas,newconfig="false"):
    uname="cisco"
    passwd="cisco"
    device = ConnectHandler(device_type='cisco_ios', ip=routerip,
username=uname, password=passwd)
    cmds=""
    cmds="router bgp "+localas
    cmds=cmds+"\n neighbor "+remoteip+" remote-as "+remoteas
    xcheck=device.send_config_set(cmds)
    print (xcheck)
    outputx=device.send_command("wr mem")
    print (outputx)
    device.disconnect()


def validatebgp(routerip,remoteip):
    uname="cisco"
    passwd="cisco"
    device = ConnectHandler(device_type='cisco_ios', ip=routerip,
username=uname, password=passwd)
    cmds="show ip bgp neighbors "+remoteip+" | include BGP state"
    outputx=device.send_command(cmds)
    if ("Established" in outputx):
        print ("Remote IP "+remoteip+" on local router "+routerip+" is in
ESTABLISHED state")
    else:
        print ("Remote IP "+remoteip+" on local router "+routerip+" is NOT
IN ESTABLISHED state")
    device.disconnect()
pushbgpconfig("192.168.255.249","192.168.255.248","200","200")
### we give some time for bgp to establish
print ("Now sleeping for 5 seconds....")
time.sleep(5) # 5 seconds
validatebgp("192.168.255.249","192.168.255.248")
```

The output is as follows:

```
Python 3.6.1 Shell
File  Edit  Shell  Debug  Options  Window  Help
Python 3.6.1 (v3.6.1:69c0db5, Mar 21 2017, 17:54:52) [MSC v.1900 32 bit (Intel)] on win32
Type "copyright", "credits" or "license()" for more information.
>>>
========================= RESTART: C:/a1/bgpconfigpush.py =========================
config term
Enter configuration commands, one per line.  End with CNTL/Z.
testrouter(config)#router bgp 200
testrouter(config-router)# neighbor 192.168.255.248 remote-as 200
testrouter(config-router)#end
testrouter#
Building configuration...
[OK]
Now sleeping for 5 seconds....
Remote IP 192.168.255.248 on local router 192.168.255.249 is in ESTABLISHED state
>>>
```

As we see, we push the neighbor config (BGP config) to the router. Once the config is pushed, the script waits for 5 seconds and validates the state of BGP if it is in the ESTABLISHED state. This validation confirms that the config that we pushed has all the sessions that are newly configured as established.

Let's push an incorrect config as follows:

```
from netmiko import ConnectHandler
import time
def pushbgpconfig(routerip,remoteip,localas,remoteas,newconfig="false"):
 uname="cisco"
 passwd="cisco"
 device = ConnectHandler(device_type='cisco_ios', ip=routerip,
username=uname, password=passwd)
 cmds=""
 cmds="router bgp "+localas
 cmds=cmds+"\n neighbor "+remoteip+" remote-as "+remoteas
 xcheck=device.send_config_set(cmds)
 print (xcheck)
 outputx=device.send_command("wr mem")
 print (outputx)
 device.disconnect()
def validatebgp(routerip,remoteip):
 uname="cisco"
 passwd="cisco"
 device = ConnectHandler(device_type='cisco_ios', ip=routerip,
username=uname, password=passwd)
 cmds="show ip bgp neighbors "+remoteip+" | include BGP state"
 outputx=device.send_command(cmds)
 if ("Established" in outputx):
```

```
    print ("Remote IP "+remoteip+" on local router "+routerip+" is in
ESTABLISHED state")
    else:
    print ("Remote IP "+remoteip+" on local router "+routerip+" is NOT IN
ESTABLISHED state")
    device.disconnect()

pushbgpconfig("192.168.255.249","192.168.255.248","200","400")
### we give some time for bgp to establish
print ("Now sleeping for 5 seconds....")
time.sleep(5) # 5 seconds
validatebgp("192.168.255.249","192.168.255.248")
```

The output of the preceding code is as follows:

```
Python 3.6.1 Shell
File  Edit  Shell  Debug  Options  Window  Help
Python 3.6.1 (v3.6.1:69c0db5, Mar 21 2017, 17:54:52) [MSC v.1900 32 bit (Intel)] on win32
Type "copyright", "credits" or "license()" for more information.
>>>
==================== RESTART: C:/a1/bgpconfigpush.py ====================
config term
Enter configuration commands, one per line.  End with CNTL/Z.
testrouter(config)#router bgp 200
testrouter(config-router)# neighbor 192.168.255.248 remote-as 400
testrouter(config-router)#end
testrouter#
Building configuration...
[OK]
Now sleeping for 5 seconds....
Remote IP 192.168.255.248 on local router 192.168.255.249 is NOT IN ESTABLISHED state
>>>
```

As we see in the preceding output, now we are pushing the config with an incorrect remote (400 in this case). Of course, since the config is not correct, we get a non-established message, which confirms that the config that we pushed was not correct. In a similar way, we can push the bulk of the configs by calling the methods as many times as we want for each of the remote neighbors to be configured. Additionally, sometimes we need to get specific information under certain config sections from a running config.

As an example, the following code will give out a list for each section of the running config:

```
from netmiko import ConnectHandler
import itertools

class linecheck:
    def __init__(self):
        self.state = 0
    def __call__(self, line):
        if line and not line[0].isspace():
            self.state += 1
        return self.state

def getbgpipaddress(routerip):
    uname="cisco"
    passwd="cisco"
    device = ConnectHandler(device_type='cisco_ios', ip=routerip,
username=uname, password=passwd)
    cmds="show running-config"
    outputx=device.send_command(cmds)
    device.disconnect()
    for _, group in itertools.groupby(outputx.splitlines(),
key=linecheck()):
        templist=list(group)
        if (len(templist) == 1):
            if "!" in str(templist):
                continue
        print(templist)


getbgpipaddress("192.168.255.249")
```

The output is as follows:

As we see in the preceding output, we got all the sections of the running config, except the exclamation mark ! that we see in a running config (executing the router command `show running-config` on router). The focus of this output is that we have a config that is now parsed for each section in running config grouped in a single list, or in other words, a specific set of configs meant for a specific section (such as an interface or BGP) is grouped in a single list.

Lets enhance this code. As an example, we only want to see what BGP remote IPs are configured in our router:

```python
from netmiko import ConnectHandler
import itertools
import re

class linecheck:
    def __init__(self):
        self.state = 0
```

```
        def __call__(self, line):
            if line and not line[0].isspace():
                self.state += 1
            return self.state

    def getbgpipaddress(routerip):
        uname="cisco"
        passwd="cisco"
        device = ConnectHandler(device_type='cisco_ios', ip=routerip,
    username=uname, password=passwd)
        cmds="show running-config"
        outputx=device.send_command(cmds)
        device.disconnect()
        for _, group in itertools.groupby(outputx.splitlines(),
    key=linecheck()):
            templist=list(group)
            if (len(templist) == 1):
                if "!" in str(templist):
                    continue
            if "router bgp" in str(templist):
                for line in templist:
                    if ("neighbor " in line):
                        remoteip=re.search("\d+.\d+.\d+.\d+",line)
                        print ("Remote ip: "+remoteip.group(0))


    getbgpipaddress("192.168.255.249")
```

The output is as follows:

```
Python 3.6.1 Shell
File  Edit  Shell  Debug  Options  Window  Help
Python 3.6.1 (v3.6.1:69c0db5, Mar 21 2017, 17:54:52) [MSC v.1900 32 bit (Intel)] on win32
Type "copyright", "credits" or "license()" for more information.
>>>
========================= RESTART: C:/a1/bgpipconfig.py =========================
Remote ip: 192.168.255.248
>>>
```

In this case, first we parse the running config and focus on the section which has the `router bgp` config. Once we get to that particular list, we parse the list and fetch the remote IP using the regex on the specific command that contains the string `neighbor`. The result values would be the remote IPs under the BGP section.

As we are working with BGP, the AS numbers, being an integral part of BGP, need to be parsed or validated. Using the preceding strategies, we can get the AS numbers for BGP routes/prefixes, but in addition to that, there is a Python library `pyasn` that can easily find out AS number information for a given public IP address.

Again, as mentioned earlier, we need to install the following library before we can call it in the code, by using:

```
pip install cymruwhois
```

The code is as follows:

```python
import socket

def getfromhostname(hostname):
    print ("AS info for hostname :"+hostname)
    ip = socket.gethostbyname(hostname)
    from cymruwhois import Client
    c=Client()
    r=c.lookup(ip)
    print (r.asn)
    print (r.owner)

def getfromip(ip):
    print ("AS info for IP : "+ip)
    from cymruwhois import Client
    c=Client()
    r=c.lookup(ip)
    print (r.asn)
    print (r.owner)


getfromhostname("google.com")
getfromip("107.155.8.0")
```

The output is as follows:

```
Python 3.6.1 Shell
File  Edit  Shell  Debug  Options  Window  Help
Python 3.6.1 (v3.6.1:69c0db5, Mar 21 2017, 17:54:52) [MSC v.1900 32 bit (Intel)] on
Type "copyright", "credits" or "license()" for more information.
>>>
================================ RESTART: C:/a1/bgpwhois.py ================================
AS info for hostname :google.com
15169
GOOGLE - Google Inc., US
AS info for IP : 107.155.8.0
3356
LEVEL3 - Level 3 Communications, Inc., US
>>>
```

As we see, the first method `getfromhostname` is used to fetch information for a given hostname. The other method `getfromip` is used to fetch the same information by using an IP address instead of any hostname.

Configuring Cisco switchport for access point

When working with a multi-device environment, along with routers and switches we need to interact with other network gear(s) like wireless devices. This example will show how to configure a switch with specific ports to be connected to **Access Point (AP)** as trunk.

In our test case, assuming the VLANs configured on AP are `vlan 100` and `vlan 200` for users, and the native VLAN is `vlan 10`, and the code is as follows:

```python
from netmiko import ConnectHandler
import time

def apvlanpush(routerip,switchport):
    uname="cisco"
    passwd="cisco"
    device = ConnectHandler(device_type='cisco_ios', ip=routerip,
username=uname, password=passwd)
    cmds="interface "+switchport
    cmds=cmds+"\nswitchport mode trunk\nswitchport trunk encapsulation
dot1q\n"
    cmds=cmds+ "switchport trunk native vlan 10\nswitchport trunk allowed
vlan add 10,100,200\nno shut\n"
    xcheck=device.send_config_set(cmds)
    print (xcheck)
    device.disconnect()
```

```
def validateswitchport(routerip,switchport):
    uname="cisco"
    passwd="cisco"
    device = ConnectHandler(device_type='cisco_ios', ip=routerip,
username=uname, password=passwd)
    cmds="show interface "+switchport+" switchport "
    outputx=device.send_command(cmds)
    print (outputx)
    device.disconnect()
apvlanpush("192.168.255.245","FastEthernet2/0")
time.sleep(5) # 5 seconds
validateswitchport("192.168.255.245","FastEthernet2/0")
```

The output is as follows:

```
Python 3.6.1 Shell
File  Edit  Shell  Debug  Options  Window  Help
Python 3.6.1 (v3.6.1:69c0db5, Mar 21 2017, 17:54:52) [MSC v.1900 32 bit (Intel)] on win32
Type "copyright", "credits" or "license()" for more information.
>>>
==================== RESTART: C:/a1/apvlanpush.py ====================
config term
Enter configuration commands, one per line.  End with CNTL/Z.
R3(config)#interface FastEthernet2/0
R3(config-if)#switchport mode trunk
R3(config-if)#switchport trunk encapsulation dot1q
R3(config-if)#switchport trunk native vlan 10
R3(config-if)#switchport trunk allowed vlan add 10,100,200
R3(config-if)#no shut
R3(config-if)#end
R3#
Name: Fa2/0
Switchport: Enabled
Administrative Mode: trunk
Operational Mode: down
Administrative Trunking Encapsulation: dot1q
Negotiation of Trunking: Disabled
Access Mode VLAN: 0 ((Inactive))
Trunking Native Mode VLAN: 10 ((Inactive))
Trunking VLANs Enabled: ALL
Trunking VLANs Active: none
Priority for untagged frames: 0
Override vlan tag priority: FALSE
Voice VLAN: none
Appliance trust: none
>>>
```

As we see, the AP needs to be connected to our switchport, which needs to be a trunk, with certain access VLANs to be allowed; hence we create two methods, the first of which passes router/switch name and the interfaces that needs to be configured.

Once the configuration is successfully pushed on the switch, we execute the `validateswitchport` method to validate if the same port is now in trunk mode. The output of the `validateswitchport` method spills out the output of the command, on which we can further introduce the regex and splits to get any specific information we want from that output (such as the `Administrative Mode` or `Operational Mode`).

As an enhancement, we can also use the outputs from the validation method to call other methods that would perform some additional configs (if required), based on the result that we got earlier. (For example, changing the `Trunking Native Mode VLAN` to 20).

Let's see the new code with the additional enhancement of changing the native VLAN to 20. The code is as follows:

```
from netmiko import ConnectHandler
import time

def apvlanpush(routerip,switchport):
    uname="cisco"
    passwd="cisco"
    device = ConnectHandler(device_type='cisco_ios', ip=routerip,
username=uname, password=passwd)
    cmds="interface "+switchport
    cmds=cmds+"\nswitchport mode trunk\nswitchport trunk encapsulation
dot1q\n"
    cmds=cmds+ "switchport trunk native vlan 10\nswitchport trunk allowed
vlan add 10,100,200\nno shut\n"
    xcheck=device.send_config_set(cmds)
    print (xcheck)
    device.disconnect()

def validateswitchport(routerip,switchport):
    print ("\nValidating switchport...."+switchport)
    uname="cisco"
    passwd="cisco"
    device = ConnectHandler(device_type='cisco_ios', ip=routerip,
username=uname, password=passwd)
    cmds="show interface "+switchport+" switchport "
    outputx=device.send_command(cmds)
    print (outputx)
    outputx=outputx.split("\n")
    for line in outputx:
        if ("Trunking Native Mode VLAN: 10" in line):
            changenativevlan(routerip,switchport,"20")
    device.disconnect()

def changenativevlan(routerip,switchport,nativevlan):
    print ("\nNow changing native VLAN on switchport",switchport)
```

```
        uname="cisco"
        passwd="cisco"
        device = ConnectHandler(device_type='cisco_ios', ip=routerip,
    username=uname, password=passwd)
        cmds="interface "+switchport
        cmds=cmds+"\nswitchport trunk native vlan "+nativevlan+"\n"
        xcheck=device.send_config_set(cmds)
        print (xcheck)
        validateswitchport(routerip,switchport)
        device.disconnect()
    apvlanpush("192.168.255.245","FastEthernet2/0")
    time.sleep(5) # 5 seconds
    validateswitchport("192.168.255.245","FastEthernet2/0")
```

The output is explained in two sections as follows:

- Validating and changing the native VLAN to 20:

```
Python 3.6.1 Shell
File Edit Shell Debug Options Window Help
Python 3.6.1 (v3.6.1:69c0db5, Mar 21 2017, 17:54:52) [MSC v.1900 32 bit (Intel)] on win32
Type "copyright", "credits" or "license()" for more information.
>>>
================= RESTART: C:/a1/apvlanpush.py =================
config term
Enter configuration commands, one per line.  End with CNTL/Z.
R3(config)#interface FastEthernet2/0
R3(config-if)#switchport mode trunk
R3(config-if)#switchport trunk encapsulation dot1q
R3(config-if)#switchport trunk native vlan 10
R3(config-if)#switchport trunk allowed vlan add 10,100,200
R3(config-if)#no shut
R3(config-if)#end
R3#

Validating switchport....FastEthernet2/0
Name: Fa2/0
Switchport: Enabled
Administrative Mode: trunk
Operational Mode: down
Administrative Trunking Encapsulation: dot1q
Negotiation of Trunking: Disabled
Access Mode VLAN: 0 ((Inactive))
Trunking Native Mode VLAN: 10 ((Inactive))
Trunking VLANs Enabled: ALL
Trunking VLANs Active: none
Priority for untagged frames: 0
Override vlan tag priority: FALSE
Voice VLAN: none
Appliance trust: none

Now changing native VLAN on switchport FastEthernet2/0
config term
Enter configuration commands, one per line.  End with CNTL/Z.
R3(config)#interface FastEthernet2/0
R3(config-if)#switchport trunk native vlan 20
R3(config-if)#end
R3#
```

- Revalidating with the new native VLAN number:

```
Validating switchport....FastEthernet2/0
Name: Fa2/0
Switchport: Enabled
Administrative Mode: trunk
Operational Mode: down
Administrative Trunking Encapsulation: dot1q
Negotiation of Trunking: Disabled
Access Mode VLAN: 0 ((Inactive))
Trunking Native Mode VLAN: 20 ((Inactive))
Trunking VLANs Enabled: ALL
Trunking VLANs Active: none
Priority for untagged frames: 0
Override vlan tag priority: FALSE
Voice VLAN: none
Appliance trust: none
>>>
```

As we see in the final validation, now we have a native VLAN 20, instead of the earlier 10. This is also a good troubleshooting technique as in multiple scenarios there are requirements of a **what if analysis** (to take decisions based upon the evaluation of a certain condition) in which we need to take some actions based on the dynamic results received. Since, here in our code we validated that the native VLAN needs to be 20, hence we performed another action to correct that earlier config.

Configuring Cisco switchport for IP Phone

Similar to the earlier scenario, where we want a switchport as a trunk port for AP, we can configure the switchport to work with IP Phones. An additional task for configuring a port to be used as IP Phone is that another end machine or data machine can be connected to the IP Phone for data transfer. In other words, a single switchport of a Cisco router can act as both a voice and data port when used with IP Phone.

Let's see an example of configuring a switchport to act as an IP Phone port:

```
from netmiko import ConnectHandler
import time

def ipphoneconfig(routerip,switchport):
    uname="cisco"
    passwd="cisco"
    device = ConnectHandler(device_type='cisco_ios', ip=routerip,
username=uname, password=passwd)
    cmds="interface "+switchport
    cmds=cmds+"\nswitchport mode access\nswitchport access vlan 100\n"
    cmds=cmds+ "switchport voice vlan 200\nspanning-tree portfast\nno
shut\n"
    xcheck=device.send_config_set(cmds)
    print (xcheck)
    device.disconnect()

def validateswitchport(routerip,switchport):
    print ("\nValidating switchport...."+switchport)
    uname="cisco"
    passwd="cisco"
    device = ConnectHandler(device_type='cisco_ios', ip=routerip,
username=uname, password=passwd)
    cmds="show interface "+switchport+" switchport "
    outputx=device.send_command(cmds)
    print (outputx)
    outputx=outputx.split("\n")
    for line in outputx:
        if ("Trunking Native Mode VLAN: 10" in line):
            changenativevlan(routerip,switchport,"20")
    device.disconnect()
ipphoneconfig("192.168.255.245","FastEthernet2/5")
time.sleep(5) # 5 seconds
validateswitchport("192.168.255.245","FastEthernet2/5")
```

The output is as follows:

```
Python 3.6.1 Shell
File  Edit  Shell  Debug  Options  Window  Help
Python 3.6.1 (v3.6.1:69c0db5, Mar 21 2017, 17:54:52) [MSC v.1900 32 bit (Intel)] on win32
Type "copyright", "credits" or "license()" for more information.
>>>
============================ RESTART: C:/a1/ipphonepush.py ============================
config term
Enter configuration commands, one per line.  End with CNTL/Z.
R3(config)#interface FastEthernet2/5
R3(config-if)#switchport mode access
R3(config-if)#switchport access vlan 100
R3(config-if)#switchport voice vlan 200
R3(config-if)#spanning-tree portfast
%Warning: portfast should only be enabled on ports connected to a single host.
 Connecting hubs, concentrators, switches,  bridges, etc.to this interface
 when portfast is enabled, can cause temporary spanning tree loops.
 Use with CAUTION

%Portfast has been configured on FastEthernet2/5 but will only
 have effect when the interface is in a non-trunking mode.
R3(config-if)#no shut
R3(config-if)#end
R3#

Validating switchport....FastEthernet2/5
Name: Fa2/5
Switchport: Enabled
Administrative Mode: static access
Operational Mode: down
Administrative Trunking Encapsulation: dot1q
Negotiation of Trunking: Disabled
Access Mode VLAN: 100 (VLAN0100)
Trunking Native Mode VLAN: 1 (default)
Trunking VLANs Enabled: ALL
Trunking VLANs Active: none
Priority for untagged frames: 0
Override vlan tag priority: FALSE
Voice VLAN: 200
Appliance trust: none
>>>
```

As we see now, the port configured (FastEthernet 2/5) has been assigned a Voice VLAN of 200 and a data/access VLAN of 100 (from the preceding output, notice the line Access Mode VLAN: 100 (VLAN0100). Any IP Phone connecting to this port will have access to both the VLANs for its voice and data usage. Again, going by previous examples, we can perform additional validations and checks on the ports and trigger some actions in case of any incorrect or missing configs.

Wireless LAN (WLAN)

There are many vendors that have backend APIs that can be controlled or called using Python to perform certain wireless tasks. A commonly used vendor in wireless is `Netgear`. Python has a library `pynetgear` that helps us achieve some of the automation to control our locally connected devices.

Let's see an example of fetching the current network devices connected to the local wireless Netgear router in our network:

```
>>> from pynetgear import Netgear, Device
>>> netgear = Netgear("myrouterpassword", "192.168.100.1","admin","80")
>>> for i in netgear.get_attached_devices():
  print (i)
```

The `Netgear` method accepts four arguments in the following order (`routerpassword`, `routerip`, `routerusername`, and `routerport`). As we see in the current example, the router is reachable using `http://192.168.100.1` with the username `admin` and password as `myrouterpassword`. Hence, we call the method with these parameters.

The output is shown as follows:

```
>>> netgear.get_attached_devices()
[Device(signal=3, ip='192.168.100.4', name='ANDROID-12345',
mac='xx:xx:xx:xx:xx:xx', type='wireless', link_rate=72),
Device(signal=None, ip='192.168.100.55', name='ANDROID-678910',
mac='yy:yy:yy:yy:yy:yy', type='wireless', link_rate=72),
Device(signal=None, ip='192.168.100.10', name='mylaptop',
mac='zz:zz:zz:zz:zz:zz', type='wireless', link_rate=520)]
```

As we see, the method `get_attached_devices()` returned a list of all the IPs, their MAC addresses (hidden in this example), signal (or wireless band being used), and the link rate for the connection in Mbps.

We can use similar type of methods to manipulate bandwidth, block any user, or perform other tasks that are exposed by the APIs of the specific hardware manufacturer.

Access of IP Address Management (IPAM)

Another requirement in networking is to use the IPAM database for IPAM. It is provided by different vendors, and as an example here, we would refer to SolarWind's IPAM. SolarWinds is again an industry standard tool for monitoring and performing various functionalities on a network, and it has a good set of APIs to interact with using its ORION SDK toolkit.

In Python, we can install the library `orionsdk` to achieve interaction with SolarWinds. Let's see an example in which we fetch the next available IP address from the IPAM module in SolarWinds:

```python
from orionsdk import SwisClient

npm_server = 'mysolarwindsserver'
username = "test"
password = "test"

verify = False
if not verify:
    from requests.packages.urllib3.exceptions import InsecureRequestWarning
    requests.packages.urllib3.disable_warnings(InsecureRequestWarning)

swis = SwisClient(npm_server, username, password)

print("My IPAM test:")
results=swis.query("SELECT TOP 1 Status, DisplayName FROM IPAM.IPNode WHERE
Status=2")
print (results)

### for a formatted printing
for row in results['results']:
 print("Avaliable: {DisplayName}".format(**row))
```

The output is as follows:

As we see in the preceding code, we use the `orionsdk` library to call the API for SolarWinds from the `mysolarwindsserver` server. The username and password needed for the SolarWinds are passed in script, and we use a simple SQL query (which is understandable by SolarWinds) which is as follows:

```
SELECT TOP 1 Status, DisplayName FROM IPAM.IPNode  WHERE Status=2
```

This query fetches the next available IP address (denoted by `Status=2` in SolarWinds) and prints it. The first print is the raw print and the one in `for` loop; it prints out the value in a better understandable format as shown in the preceding output.

Example and use case

Here, we will see a detailed example that is common to most network engineers, and how to automate it using Python. Also, we will create it as a web based tool, enabling it to run from any environment or machine, using only a browser.

Create a web-based pre and post check tool for validations

In the following example, we will see how we can perform a pre and post check on any network maintenance that we do. This is generally required by every network engineer while performing activities on production devices to ensure that once the maintenance activity is complete, an engineer has not missed out anything that could cause an issue later on. It is also required to validate if our changes and maintenance have been completed successfully, or if we need to perform additional fixes and rollbacks in case of validations that have failed.

The following are the steps to create and execute the tool:

Step 1 – Create the main HTML file

We will design a web-based form to select certain show commands that we will call for performing checks. These commands, when executed, will act as a precheck; once our maintenance activity is complete, we will act again as a postcheck.

Any difference between the same command outputs in precheck or postcheck scenarios will be highlighted and the engineer will be in a good position to make decisions on calling the maintenance a success or failure, based on the outputs.

The HTML code (prepostcheck.html) is as follows:

```html
<!DOCTYPE html>

<html xmlns="http://www.w3.org/1999/xhtml">
<head>
        <script>
            function checkme() {
    var a=document.forms["search"]["cmds"].value;
    var b=document.forms["search"]["searchbox"].value;
    var c=document.forms["search"]["prepost"].value;
    var d=document.forms["search"]["changeid"].value;
    if (a==null || a=="")
    {
      alert("Please Fill All Fields");
      return false;
    }
    if (b==null || b=="")
    {
      alert("Please Fill All Fields");
      return false;
    }
    if (c==null || c=="")
    {
      alert("Please Fill All Fields");
      return false;
    }
    if (d==null || d=="")
    {
      alert("Please Fill All Fields");
      return false;
    }
            document.getElementById("mypoint").style.display =
    "inline";
```

```
            }
    </script>
    </head>
    <body>
    <h2> Pre/Post check selection </h2>
    <form name="search" action="checks.py" method="post"
    onsubmit="return checkme()">
    Host IP: (Multiple IPs seperated by comma)<br><input type="text"
    name="searchbox" size='80' required>
    <p></p>
    Commands (Select):
    <br>
    <select name="cmds" multiple style="width:200px;height:200px;"
    required>
      <option value="show version">show version</option>
      <option value="show ip int brief">show ip int brief</option>
      <option value="show interface description">show interface
    description</option>
      <option value="show clock">show clock</option>
      <option value="show log">show log (last 100)</option>
      <option value="show run">show run</option>
      <option value="show ip bgp summary">show ip bgp summary</option>
      <option value="show ip route">show ip route</option>
      <option value="show ip route summary">show ip route
    summary</option>
      <option value="show ip ospf">show ip ospf</option>
      <option value="show interfaces status">show interfaces
    status</option>
    </select>
    <p></p>
    Mantainence ID: <input type="text" name="changeid" required>
    <p></p>
    Pre/Post: <br>
    <input type="radio" name="prepost" value="pre" checked>
    Precheck<br>
    <input type="radio" name="prepost" value="post"> Postcheck<br>
    <p></p>
    <input type="submit" value="Submit">
    <br><br><br>
    </form>
    <p><label id="mypoint" style="display: none;background-color:
    yellow;"><b>Please be Patient.... Gathering
    results!!!</b></label></p>
    </body>
    </html>
```

This will create the main page on which we select our initial options (set of commands and if we need to perform a precheck or a postcheck). The output is as follows:

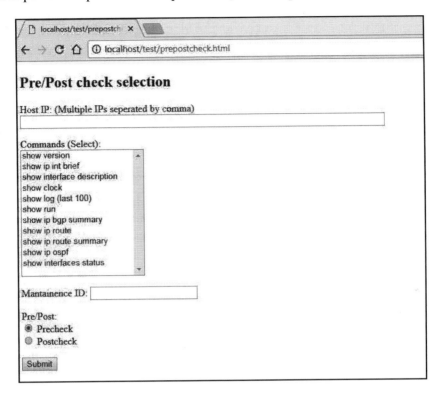

Main page

An additional JavaScript code in HTML ensures that the Submit button will not send any data until all the selections are made. There is no point sending data which is not completed; for example, if we do not fill out entire fields the Submit option will not proceed, giving out the message that we see in the following screenshot:

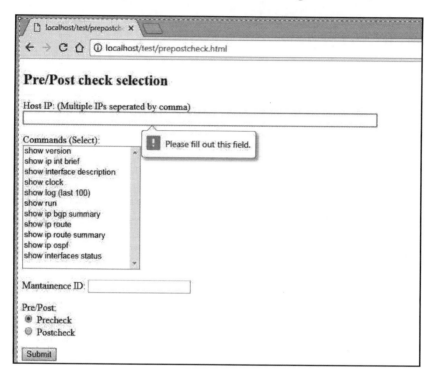

Unless all the fields are not filled, hitting the Submit button will spill out this message and the code will not continue. Additionally, as we see in the code, the Submit button is tied to the Python script, with checks.py as a POST method. In other words, the selections we will make will be sent to checks.py as a POST method.

Step 2 – Create the backend Python code

Now, let's see the back end Python code (checks.py) that will accept these inputs from HTML form and perform its task. The code is as follows:

```
#!/usr/bin/env python
import cgi
import paramiko
import time
```

```
import re
import sys
import os
import requests
import urllib
import datetime
from datetime import datetime
from threading import Thread
from random import randrange

form = cgi.FieldStorage()
searchterm = form.getvalue('searchbox')
cmds = form.getvalue('cmds')
changeid = form.getvalue('changeid')
prepost=form.getvalue('prepost')
searchterm=searchterm.split(",")
xval=""
xval=datetime.now().strftime("%Y-%m-%d_%H_%M_%S")

returns = {}
def getoutput(devip,cmd):
    try:
        output=""
        mpath="C:/iistest/logs/"
        fname=changeid+"_"+devip+"_"+prepost+"_"+xval+".txt"
        fopen=open(mpath+fname,"w")
        remote_conn_pre = paramiko.SSHClient()
remote_conn_pre.set_missing_host_key_policy(paramiko.AutoAddPolicy())
        remote_conn_pre.connect(devip, username='cisco', password='cisco',
look_for_keys=False, allow_agent=False)
        remote_conn = remote_conn_pre.invoke_shell()
        remote_conn.settimeout(60)
        command=cmd
        remote_conn.send(command+"\n")
        time.sleep(15)
        output=(remote_conn.recv(250000)).decode()
        fopen.write(output)
        remote_conn.close()
        fopen.close()
        returns[devip]=("Success: <a
href='http://localhost/test/logs/"+fname+"' target='_blank'>"+fname +"</a>
Created")
    except:
        returns[devip]="Error. Unable to fetch details"

try:
    xtmp=""
    cmdval="terminal length 0\n"
```

```
        if (str(cmds).count("show") > 1):
            for cmdvalue in cmds:
                if ("show" in cmdvalue):
                    if ("show log" in cmdvalue):
                        cmdvalue="terminal shell\nshow log | tail 100"
                    cmdval=cmdval+cmdvalue+"\n\n"
        else:
            if ("show" in cmds):
                if ("show log" in cmds):
                    cmds="terminal shell\nshow log | tail 100"
                cmdval=cmdval+cmds+"\n\n"
        threads_imagex= []
        for devip in searchterm:
            devip=devip.strip()
            t = Thread(target=getoutput, args=(devip,cmdval,))
            t.start()
            time.sleep(randrange(1,2,1)/20)
            threads_imagex.append(t)
        for t in threads_imagex:
            t.join()
        print("Content-type: text/html")
        print()
        xval=""
        for key in returns:
            print ("<b>"+key+"</b>:"+returns[key]+"<br>")
        print ("<br>Next step: <a
href='http://localhost/test/selectfiles.aspx'> Click here to compare files
</a>")
        print ("<br>Next step: <a
href='http://localhost/test/prepostcheck.html'> Click here to perform
pre/post check </a>")

except:
    print("Content-type: text/html")
    print()
    print("Error fetching details. Need manual validation")
    print ("<br>Next step: <a
href='http://localhost/test/selectfiles.aspx'> Click here to compare files
</a>")
    print ("<br>Next step: <a
href='http://localhost/test/prepostcheck.html'> Click here to perform
pre/post check </a>")
```

This code accepts input from a web page using the CGI parameter. Various values from the web page are parsed into the variables using the following code snippet:

```
form = cgi.FieldStorage()
searchterm = form.getvalue('searchbox')
cmds = form.getvalue('cmds')
changeid = form.getvalue('changeid')
prepost=form.getvalue('prepost')
```

Once we have these values, the additional logic is to log in into the given device(s) using the paramiko library, fetch the output of the show commands, and save it in a file under the logs folder with the output. An important aspect to note here is the way we are constructing the filename:

```
#xval=datetime.now().strftime("%Y-%m-%d_%H_%M_%S")
#and
#fname=changeid+"_"+devip+"_"+prepost+"_"+xval+".txt"
```

The fname is the filename into which we would write the output, but the filename is built dynamically with the inputs provided by the maintenance ID, device IP, pre/post status, and the time the file was created. This is to ensure that we know the device for which we are performing a pre or a post check, and at what time the file was created, to ensure we have a correct pre and post check combination.

The function getoutput() is invoked from a thread (in a multi-threaded function call) to fetch the output and store it in the newly created file. A multi-threading process is called, because if we want to perform pre or post checks in multiple devices, we can provide a comma separated IP address list in web, and Python script will in parallel invoke the show commands on all devices and create multiple pre or post check files, based on hostnames.

Let's create a `precheck` file for some commands in our example, where we fill in some values and click on the `Submit` button:

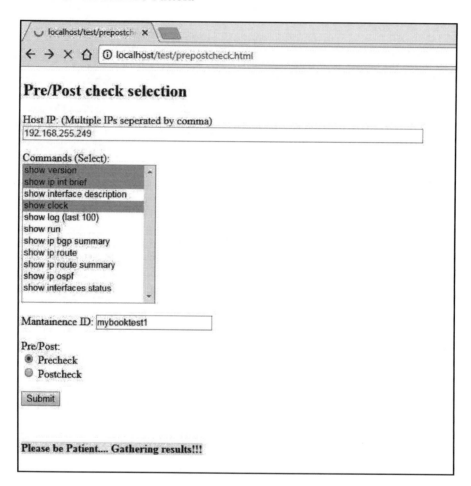

 While the gathering of data is in progress, the yellow message will be displayed to confirm that the back end work is going on.

Once the task is completed, this is what we see (as returned from the Python code):

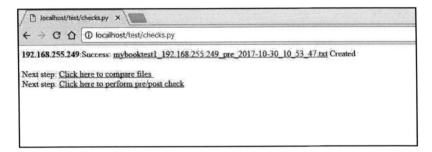

As we see, the code returns a success, which means that it was able to fetch the output of the commands that we want to validate. The filename is dynamically created, based on our selection on the main page.

A click on the .txt filename that is generated as a clickable URL (which can be used to reconfirm if we got the correct output of commands we selected earlier), shows the following output:

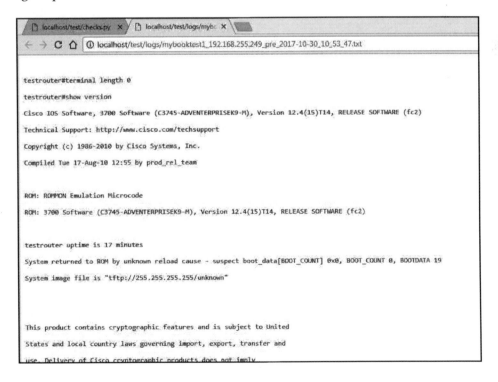

Now, let's perform the same steps and create a postcheck file.

We go back to the main page, and keeping the other values the same, we just select the radio button to Postcheck instead of Precheck. Do ensure that we select the same set of commands, since a pre and post check only make sense if we have the same data to work with:

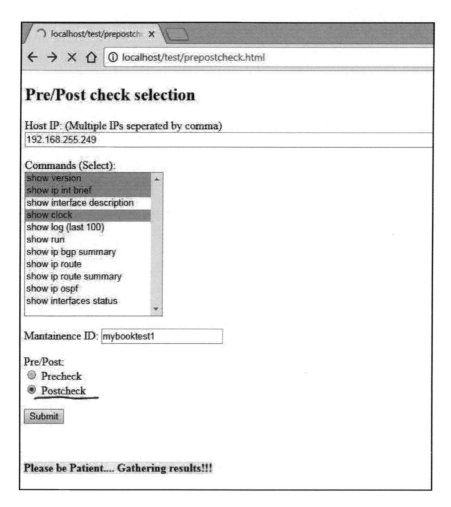

In a similar way, once the backend execution completes, we have a postcheck file created as follows:

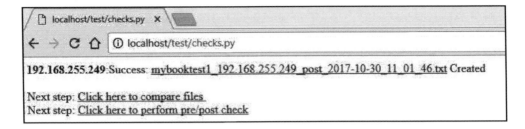

Notice the filename, the timestamp, and the `post` word changes based on our selection.

Step 3 – Create web server based files for the tool

Now with the both pre and post check files created, let's create a web framework to perform web-based pre/post check for the files. We need to create a web page in which our current log files are visible as pre and post files, and we can select the `precheck` file and its relevant `postcheck` file for comparison. As we know that we cannot use HTML or browser languages to fetch information about any files from the server, we need to use some backed web language to perform this function for us. We take advantage of ASP and VB.NET to create the web page to display the already created log files for selection and comparison.

The backend code for `selectfiles.aspx` is as follows (this is to display the files from the log directory on a browser):

```
<%@ Page Language="VB" AutoEventWireup="false"
CodeFile="selectfiles.aspx.vb" Inherits="selectfiles" %>

<!DOCTYPE html>

<html xmlns="http://www.w3.org/1999/xhtml">
<head runat="server">
    <title></title>
</head>
<body>
    <form id="form1" method="post" action="comparefiles.aspx" >
    <div>
    <%response.write(xmystring.tostring())%>
    </div>
        <input type="submit" value="Submit">
    </form>
  <br><br><br>
</body>
</html>
```

The VB.NET backend code, to fill in the values on the preceding `.aspx` page `selectfiles.aspx.vb`, is as follows:

```
Imports System.IO
Partial Class selectfiles
    Inherits System.Web.UI.Page
    Public xmystring As New StringBuilder()
  Public tableval As New Hashtable
    Protected Sub Page_Load(sender As Object, e As EventArgs) Handles
Me.Load
        Dim precheck As New List(Of String)
        Dim postcheck As New List(Of String)
        Dim prename = New SortedList
        Dim postname = New SortedList
        Dim infoReader As System.IO.FileInfo
    Dim rval as Integer
    rval=0
        xmystring.Clear()
        Dim xval As String
    Dim di As New DirectoryInfo("C:\iistest\logs\")
    Dim lFiles As FileInfo() = di.GetFiles("*.txt")
    Dim fi As System.IO.FileSystemInfo
    Dim files() As String = IO.Directory.GetFiles("C:\iistest\logs\",
"*.txt", SearchOption.TopDirectoryOnly)
    xmystring.Append("<head><style
type='text/css'>a:hover{background:blue;color:yellow;}</style></head>")
        xmystring.Append("<fieldset style='float: left;width: 49%;display:
inline-block;box-sizing: border-box;'>")
        xmystring.Append("<legend>Pre check files (Sorted by Last Modified
Date)</legend>")

        For Each fi In lFiles
    rval=rval+1
    tableval.add(fi.LastWriteTime.ToString()+rval.tostring(),fi.Name)
            'infoReader = My.Computer.FileSystem.GetFileInfo(file)
        If (fi.Name.Contains("pre")) Then
            precheck.Add(fi.LastWriteTime.ToString()+rval.tostring())
        Else
            postcheck.Add(fi.LastWriteTime.ToString()+rval.tostring())
        End If
    Next
    precheck.Sort()
    postcheck.Sort()

    xval = ""
    Dim prekey As ICollection = prename.Keys
    Dim postkey As ICollection = postname.Keys
    Dim dev As String
```

```
    Dim fnameval as String
        For Each dev In precheck
            infoReader = My.Computer.FileSystem.GetFileInfo(tableval(dev))
fnameval="http://localhost/test/logs/"+Path.GetFileName(tableval(dev))
            xval = "<input type = 'radio' name='prechecklist'
value='C:\iistest\logs\" + tableval(dev) + "' required><a href='" &
fnameval & "' target='blank'>" & tableval(dev) & "</a> ( <b>" &
dev.Substring(0,dev.LastIndexOf("M")).Trim() + "M</b>)<br>"
        xmystring.Append(xval)
        Next
    xmystring.Append("</fieldset>")
            xmystring.Append("<fieldset style='float: right;width:
49%;display: inline-block;box-sizing: border-box;'>")
        xmystring.Append("<legend>Post check files (Sorted by Last Modified
Date)</legend>")
            For Each dev In postcheck
        fnameval="http://localhost/test/logs/"+tableval(dev)
            xval = "<input type = 'radio' name='postchecklist'
value='C:\iistest\logs\" + tableval(dev) + "' required><a href='" &
fnameval & "' target='blank'>" & tableval(dev) & "</a> ( <b>" &
dev.Substring(0,dev.LastIndexOf("M")).Trim() + "M</b>)<br>"
            xmystring.Append(xval)
        Next
        xmystring.Append("</fieldset>")

    End Sub
End Class
```

This code is used to fetch the files from the log directory, and based on their filenames, they are divided into either `precheck` files or `postcheck` files. Also, the files are ordered in chronological order for easy selection during the comparison process.

Let's see the output of this page now:

Step 4 – Create server based files for pre and post files comparison

The final step is to create a web page that retrieves the text from these files and also provides frontend (or a web-based tool) for easy comparison. For our purpose, we use a JScript library called `diffview`. To call this dependency, we need to download `diffview.js`, `difflib.js`, and `diffview.css` which available here: `https://github.com/cemerick/jsdifflib`, and copy the files into our web server folder. Once done, in the similar way as accessing the files, we would again create a `.aspx` page to get the content of the selected files and display it for comparison.

The following is the code of the main page `comparefiles.aspx`:

```
<%@ Page Language="VB" AutoEventWireup="false"
CodeFile="comparefiles.aspx.vb" Inherits="comparefiles" %>

<!DOCTYPE html>

<html xmlns="http://www.w3.org/1999/xhtml">
<head>
  <meta charset="utf-8"/>
  <meta http-equiv="X-UA-Compatible" content="IE=Edge,chrome=1"/>
  <link rel="stylesheet" type="text/css" href="diffview.css"/>
  <script type="text/javascript" src="diffview.js"></script>
  <script type="text/javascript" src="difflib.js"></script>
<style type="text/css">
body {
  font-size: 12px;
  font-family: Sans-Serif;
}
h2 {
  margin: 0.5em 0 0.1em;
  text-align: center;
}
.top {
  text-align: center;
}
.textInput {
  display: block;
  width: 49%;
  float: left;
}
textarea {
  width:100%;
  height:300px;
}
```

```css
label:hover {
  text-decoration: underline;
  cursor: pointer;
}
.spacer {
  margin-left: 10px;
}
.viewType {
  font-size: 16px;
  clear: both;
  text-align: center;
  padding: 1em;
}
#diffoutput {
  width: 100%;
}
</style>

<script type="text/javascript">

function diffUsingJS(viewType) {
  "use strict";
  var byId = function (id) { return document.getElementById(id); },
    base = difflib.stringAsLines(byId("baseText").value),
    newtxt = difflib.stringAsLines(byId("newText").value),
    sm = new difflib.SequenceMatcher(base, newtxt),
    opcodes = sm.get_opcodes(),
    diffoutputdiv = byId("diffoutput"),
    contextSize = byId("contextSize").value;

  diffoutputdiv.innerHTML = "";
  contextSize = contextSize || null;

  diffoutputdiv.appendChild(diffview.buildView({
    baseTextLines: base,
    newTextLines: newtxt,
    opcodes: opcodes,
    baseTextName: "Base Text",
    newTextName: "New Text",
    contextSize: contextSize,
    viewType: viewType
  }));
}

</script>
</head>
<body>
  <div class="top">
```

```
      <strong>Context size (optional):</strong> <input type="text"
  id="contextSize" value="" />
    </div>
    <div class="textInput">
      <h2>Pre check</h2>
      <textarea id="baseText" runat="server" readonly></textarea>
    </div>
    <div class="textInput spacer">
      <h2>Post check</h2>
      <textarea id="newText" runat="server" readonly></textarea>
    </div>
      <% Response.Write(xmystring.ToString()) %>
    <div class="viewType">
      <input type="radio" name="_viewtype" id="sidebyside"
  onclick="diffUsingJS(0);" /> <label for="sidebyside">Side by Side
  Diff</label>
         
      <input type="radio" name="_viewtype" id="inline"
  onclick="diffUsingJS(1);" /> <label for="inline">Inline Diff</label>
    </div>
    <div id="diffoutput"> </div>

  </body>
  </html>
```

The backend code for the main page, to get the contents of the file (`comparefiles.aspx.vb`), is as follows:

```
Imports System.IO

Partial Class comparefiles
    Inherits System.Web.UI.Page
    Public xmystring As New StringBuilder()

    Protected Sub Page_Load(sender As Object, e As EventArgs) Handles
  Me.Load
        Dim fp As StreamReader
        Dim precheck As New List(Of String)
        Dim postcheck As New List(Of String)
        xmystring.Clear()
        Dim prefile As String
        Dim postfile As String
        prefile = Request.Form("prechecklist")
        postfile = Request.Form("postchecklist")
        fp = File.OpenText(prefile)
        baseText.InnerText = fp.ReadToEnd()
        fp = File.OpenText(postfile)
        newText.InnerText = fp.ReadToEnd()
```

```
        fp.Close()

    End Sub

End Class
```

With this ready, let's compare the files and see the results. We select the pre and post check files and click on `Submit`:

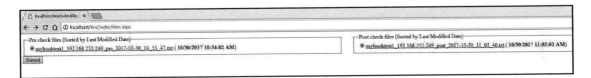

The next page takes us to the content and comparison:

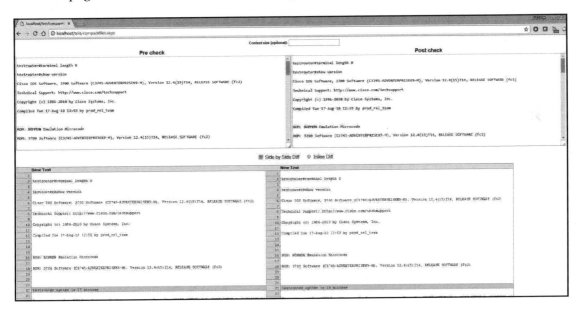

As we see in the preceding screenshot, on the left, we have the `precheck` file, and on the right, we have the `postcheck` file. Both can be read on the page itself through slides on both windows. The bottom window appears when we select either `Side by Side Diff` or `Inline Diff`.

On a `Side by Side Diff`, anything that is different will be highlighted. In our case it was uptime that was different. For everything else in common, no color highlighting will be in place and an engineer can safely assume the same states for non highlighted colors.

Let's see the same example with a `Inline Diff` comparison selection:

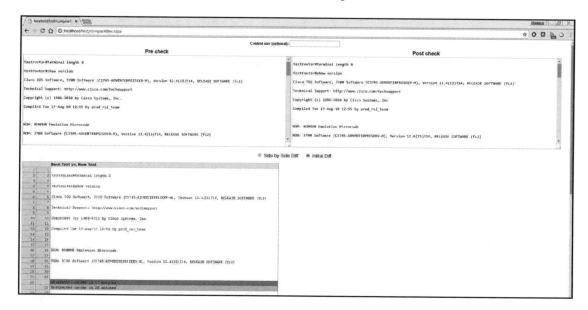

It is the same result; different lines are highlighted in different colors to confirm the pre and post check differences. With this tool now, an engineer can quickly parse through the entire log files, and based on the highlighted differences (a mismatch between `precheck` file content and `postcheck` file content), can make the decision to call the task a success or a failure.

Summary

In this chapter, we saw various concepts related to the usage of automation in daily network scenarios. We got familiar with examples of performing various tasks related to additional devices such as wireless AP and IP Phones. Additionally, we also got introduced to IPAM of SolarWinds and how to work on the API using Python.

We also saw a real-world example of creating a pre and post validation tool to help engineers make quick maintenance validation decisions, and also ported to the web so that the tool can be used from anywhere, instead of running from individual machines with Python installed as a prerequisite.

Finally, in our concluding chapter, we will look at some additional aspects of SDN to understand better usage and how and where to automate, with respect to SDN scenarios.

7
SDN Concepts in Network Automation

As we have seen on our journey so far, there are numerous scenarios where we can automate a network, from daily or routine tasks, to managing infrastructure from a single controller-based architecture. Building upon those concepts, we will now gain some additional insights for working in **software-defined networks** (**SDNs**) and look at some examples of working with cloud platforms.

Some of the key components we are going to cover are:

- Cloud platform automation
- Network automation tools
- Controller-based network fabric
- Programmable network devices

Managing cloud platforms

We can use network automation techniques through Python to work on various cloud providers. From working on cloud instances, to spinning up new VMs, controlling full access like ACLs, and creating specific network layer tasks like VPNs, and network configurations of each instance, we can automate just about anything using available connectors or APIs in Python. Let's see some basic configuration and connections on the most popular cloud platform, **Amazon Web Services** (**AWS**) using Python.

AWS provides an extensive API through its SDK called Boto 3. Boto 3 provides two types of APIs to be used, a low-level API set that is used to interact with direct AWS services, and a high-layer Python friendly API set for quick interactions with AWS. Along with Boto 3, we also would need to have the AWS CLI that is used as a **command-line interface** (**CLI**) to interact with AWS from the local machine. Think of this as a CLI based tool that is equally like DOS is to Windows from a CLI perspective.

The installation of both the AWS CLI and Boto 3 is done using `pip`:

- To install from AWS CLI, use the following command:

```
pip install awscli
```

- To install from Boto 3, use the following command:

```
pip install boto3
```

Once installed, the packages are ready to use. However, we need to configure an access key in the AWS Web Management Console which will have a certain level of restrictions (that we will define while creating the access key).

Let's quickly set up a new access key to manage the AWS in Python from our local machine:

1. Log in to the AWS web console and select **IAM** as the option:

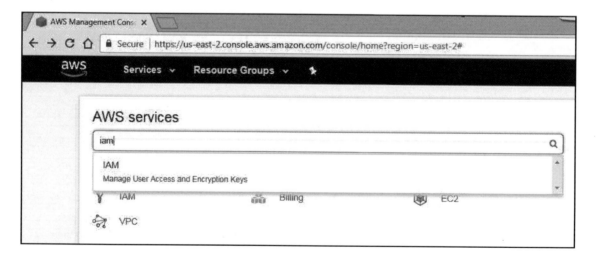

2. Click on **Add user** to create a username and password pair shown as follows:

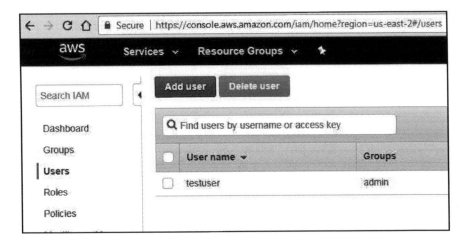

3. Select username and ensure to check **Programmatic access** to get the access ID and secret key to be used in our Python calls:

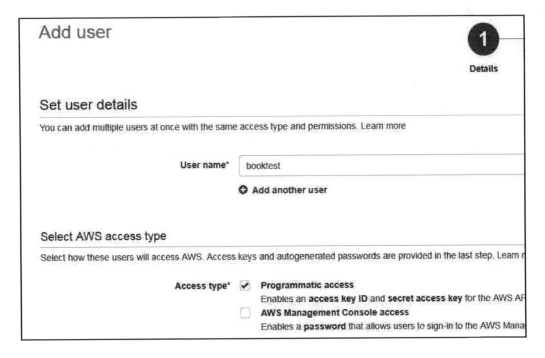

4. We also need the user to be part of a certain group (for security restrictions). In our case we make it part of the admin group which has full rights on the AWS instance:

5. If we made our selections correctly, a user is created with the username we selected (booktest) with an access key and a secret access key:

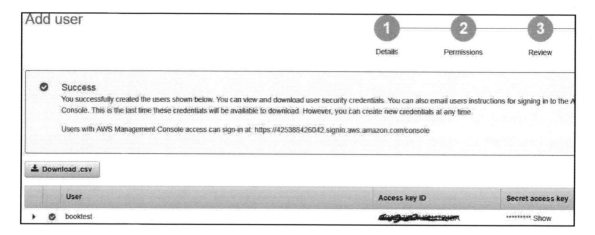

6. Once we have this key, we go back to our Python installation and on the Command Prompt, call the AWS CLI command `aws configure`:

```
C:\Windows\system32\cmd.exe

Microsoft Windows [Version 6.1.7601]
Copyright (c) 2009 Microsoft Corporation.  All rights reserved.

C:\Users\abhishek.ratan>aws configure
AWS Access Key ID [****************GC4A]:
AWS Secret Access Key [****************VmSm]:
Default region name [us-east-2]:
Default output format [json]:

C:\Users\abhishek.ratan>
```

7. As per the questions asked, we fetch the values from the AWS web console and paste them in the CLI. The final question of `Default output format` can be `text` or `json`. However, for our purpose of automation and working with Python, we would select `json` instead of `text`.

Once we are done with this backend configuration, we are ready to test our scripts by calling the Boto 3 API in Python.

Let's see an example of getting all running instances on the current AWS account for which we have the key:

```
import boto3
ec2 = boto3.resource('ec2')
for instance in ec2.instances.all():
    print (instance)
    print (instance.id, instance.state)
```

Since we have already configured the backend credentials and key with the `aws configure` CLI command, we do not need to specify any credentials in our scripts.

The output of the preceding code is as follows:

```
Python 3.6.1 Shell
File  Edit  Shell  Debug  Options  Window  Help
Python 3.6.1 (v3.6.1:69c0db5, Mar 21 2017, 17:54:52) [MSC v.190
 on win32
Type "copyright", "credits" or "license()" for more information
>>>
===================== RESTART: C:\a1\checkaws.py ========
ec2.Instance(id='i-036213d00a2891480')
i-036213d00a2891480 {'Code': 16, 'Name': 'running'}
ec2.Instance(id='i-04e997e0366f01090')
i-04e997e0366f01090 {'Code': 16, 'Name': 'running'}
>>>
```

As we see in the preceding output, we get back two instances which are EC2 instances with their instance IDs. Additionally, we also get some other parameters for the currently configured instances. In some cases, if we do not want to use the current preconfigured keys, we can call the Python program by passing the values directly into Boto 3 functions as follows:

```
import boto3

aws_access_key_id = 'accesskey'
aws_secret_access_key = 'secretaccesskey'
region_name = 'us-east-2'

ec2 =
boto3.client('ec2',aws_access_key_id=aws_access_key_id,aws_secret_access_ke
y=aws_secret_access_key,region_name=region_name)
```

Let's see another example of fetching the private IP address and instance ID for each of the instances:

```
import boto3

ec2 = boto3.client('ec2')
response = ec2.describe_instances()
for item in response['Reservations']:
    for eachinstance in item['Instances']:
        print (eachinstance['InstanceId'],eachinstance['PrivateIpAddress'])
```

The preceding code gives the following output:

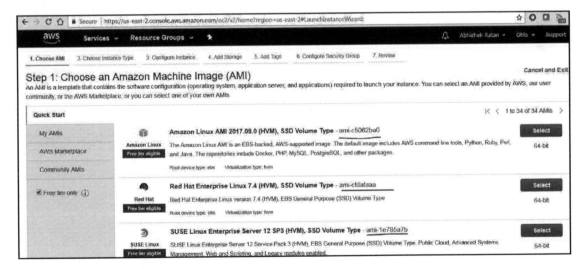

Using the Boto 3 API, we can also spin up new instances in our subscription. Let's see a final example of spinning up a new **Virtual Machine(VM)** with EC2 using Boto 3.

Before we call the Python to spin a new VM, we need to select which **Amazon Machine Image (AMI)** image to use for the instance. To find out the AMI image value, we need to open AMI in the AWS web console shown as follows:

Once we have finalized the AMI, we call the easy part, spinning the new VM:

```
import boto3
ec2 = boto3.resource('ec2')
ec2.create_instances(ImageId='amid-imageid', MinCount=1, MaxCount=5)
```

It will take some time for the script to execute, and the result value would be the instance with all its configured parameters based upon the AMI image ID selected. Similarly, we can spin up various type of instances or even new security filters using Boto 3 and ensure we have cloud controlling automation in place.

Programmable network devices

Looking back at historic implementations, we had a fixed set of hardware or networks geared for catering services to the end users. End users also had a limited set of connection options to access a limited set of networks or connected resources. As the number of users increased, a simple solution was to add additional hardware or network gear. However, with the surge of different end user devices, such as mobile phones, and high data demand and up time requirements for end users, managing the increasing amount of hardware and additional connections becomes a complex task.

A simple device failure or cable failure might impact the entire set of connected hardware or network gears, which would create a widespread downtime for end users, resulting in a loss of man hours both in terms of productivity and trust. Think of a large **internet service provider (ISP)** with recurring outages, with each outage affecting a large set of both enterprise and home users. If a new ISP were to enter the market with reliability as its unique selling point, people would not think twice before jumping to the new provider. Effectively, this could result in a loss of business and ultimately, a closure situation for the earlier provider because of the decreasing reliability and trust among its current set of users.

To handle this type of situation, one solution that has emerged is the usability of the same set of devices or network hardware to perform different functions using the same hardware platform. This has been made possible through a combination of SDN and **programmable networks (PNs)**.

SDN takes care of control plane configurations for data to automatically reroute to a path that is the best available for a specific source to the destination. For example, let's say we need to reach destination D from source A. The best path to reach D is A -> C -> D.

Now, in the case of legacy traffic flow, unless C is down or practically shut, the traffic will not flow from A -> B -> D (unless special complex configurations are done on each network gear/device). In an SDN environment, using OpenFlow as the underlying protocol, the controller will detect any issues in the path of A -> C -> D, and based upon certain issues (like packet drop or congestion in the path), would make an intelligent decision to ensure there is a new path for the data to flow from A -> B -> D.

As we see in this case, even with no physical issues on C, SDN already takes care of identifying the best path for the data to flow on, which effectively results in the best achievable performance for end users with reliability.

PN is an addition which is a collection of hardware devices in the network layer that can be programmed to behave in a different way based upon the requirements. Think of a switch acting as a router by changing its functionality through a written piece of code. Let's say we get an influx of new end users and we need to have a high switching capacity in the network layer. Some of the devices can now act as a switch rather than a router. This ensures a two-fold benefit:

- Using the same set of hardware based upon the demand and requirements, the hardware can be reused to handle new scenarios without introducing more complexity into the network by adding an additional set of hardware.
- Better control over the flow of traffic with the additional capability of securing traffic through the same set of devices. This is introduced by adding ACLs for traffic to flow from a certain set of devices, and even ensuring that a device handles only a particular type of traffic and sends the remaining traffic to other devices that are specifically programmed to handle that particular traffic. Think of it, as video with voice traffic going from a different set of devices to ensure optimal performance and load on specific devices using the same set of hardware that we currently have.

A major component of PNs (the collective name for programmable network devices), is the use of APIs that are provided by various network vendors like Cisco, Arista, and Juniper. By calling these APIs we can ensure that each of the devices from specific vendors can easily talk to each other (exchange information is a unified format), and can change the behavior of a specific hardware based upon the API calls. One example that is common in today's market is Cisco Nexus 9000 series devices. These are modular or fixed switches (with different variations), and by using OpenFlow gives us the ability to programmatically alter their behavior based upon dynamic requirements.

Taking this switch as an example, direct access to **application-specific integrated circuit (ASIC)** chip-level programming is also exposed, which ensures that the ASICs can also be programmed based upon the requirement along with the software-level variations. With SDN in place, controllers can take advantage of OpenFlow and the APIs exposed on these switches to control the role of these switches.

Cisco also provides a **Power on Auto Provisioning (PoAP)** feature to multiple devices (primarily on the Nexus platform) that helps achieve auto provisioning and commissioning as soon as a new device boots. A basic overview of this process is, if a Nexus device with the PoAP feature enabled boots and is unable to find any startup config, it locates a **Dynamic Host Configuration Protocol (DHCP)** server in the network and bootstraps using the IP address and DNS information obtained from that DHCP server. It also fetches a customized script that is executed on the device that has instructions to download and install the relevant software image files and specific configurations for that device.

A big advantage of this type of feature is that we can spin up new devices within one to two minutes by just powering it up and connecting it to a network which has DHCP functionality to fetch relevant information to new devices in the network. Think of the legacy way of bringing a router live with multiple hours of human intervention versus the current way of booting up a router, and the router taking care of itself without any human intervention.

Similarly, using the APIs (**NX-API** is the underlying terminology used for **Nexus API**), better visibility in terms of packet flow and monitoring is also being exposed from Cisco, and, using simple scripts written in any language (like Python), the path and flow of traffic can be modified based upon the results returned back through the call of those APIs.

Taking another example, we have network device vendor Arista. Arista has introduced Arista **Extensible Operating System (EOS)**, which is a highly modular and Linux-based network OS. Using Arista EOS, managing multiple devices becomes easy as it has the ability to provide extensive APIs (Linux kernel-based and additional ones related to Arista), and call APIs for various vendors to configure and deploy numerous end nodes. A feature introduced by Arista called **Smart System Upgrade (SSU)**, ensures that as we perform OS upgrades on Arista devices, it restarts its services with the upgraded OS versions but without rebooting to ensure minimal traffic interruption during upgrades. These features ensure that we have resiliency and up time even when we have new patches and OS upgrades rolled out on the data centers or multiple devices at once.

Arista EOS provides extended functionality for the devices to be managed through APIs by providing a set of APIs call **eAPI**. eAPI can be used to configure Arista devices by calling the eAPI framework from any scripting or programmable language. Let's see a very basic example of how to manage an Arista switch using eAPI.

We need to configure eAPI on the Arista switch:

```
Arista> enable
Arista# configure terminal
Arista(config)# management api http-commands
Arista(config-mgmt-api-http-cmds)# no shutdown
```

```
Arista(config-mgmt-api-http-cmds)# protocol http
Arista(config-mgmt-api-http-cmds)#end
```

This ensures that the Arista eAPI functionality is enabled on the router, and we can use HTTP protocol to interact with the API. We can also switch between the options of eAPI available over HTTPS, by using the command `protocol https`.

To verify if our configuration is correct, we use the command `show management api http-commands`, as follows:

```
Arista# show management api http-commands
Enabled: Yes
HTTPS server: shutdown, set to use port 443
HTTP server: running, set to use port 80
```

We can check if the eAPI framework is now accessible using the browser command `http://<ip of router>`.

A couple of examples from Arista depict the output that we get using the URL (in this case we have HTTPS enabled instead of HTTP):

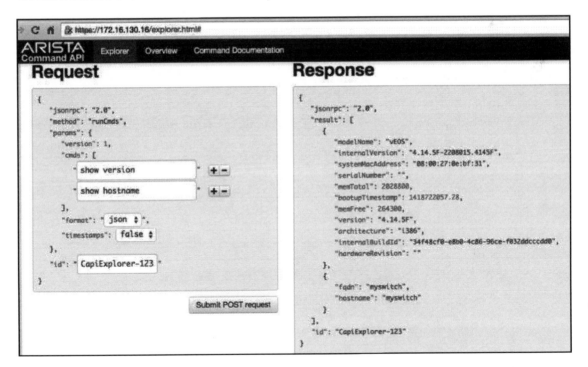

Here we see a set of commands passed (`show version` and `show hostname`), and the response from the API confirms the result set. Additionally, the **Command Response Documentation** tab shows us the available APIs that can be used for reference:

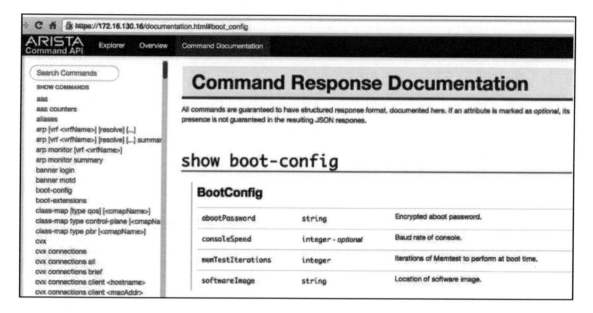

Let's see how to call the same in Python:

As a prerequisite we need to install `jsonrpclib`, which can be found at URL `https://pypi.python.org/pypi/jsonrpclib`. This is used to parse the **remote procedure call** (RPC) in JSON format. Once done, the following code will result in the same set of values that we got using the browser:

```
from jsonrpclib import Server
switch = Server( "https://admin:admin@172.16.130.16/command-api" )
response = switch.runCmds( 1, [ "show hostname" ] )
print ("Hello, my name is: ", response[0][ "hostname" ] )
response = switch.runCmds( 1, [ "show version" ] )
print ("My MAC address is: ", response[0][ "systemMacAddress" ] )
print ("My version is: ", response[0][ "version" ])
```

The preceding code gives the following output:

```
Hello, my name is: Arista
My MAC address is: 08:00:27:0e:bf:31
My version is: 4.14.5F
```

In a similar way, Arista has also introduced a library for Python that can be used as an alternate to `jsonrpclib`. The library `pyeapi`, which can be found at URL `https://pypi.python.org/pypi/pyeapi`, is a Python wrapper for the Arista EOS eAPI. Going by the example, here is how we can access the same set of devices using `pyeapi`.

From the developer page, here is an example that depicts how we can use `pyeapi` for API handling on Arista:

```
>>> from pprint import pprint as pp
>>> node = pyeapi.connect(transport='https', host='veos03',
username='eapi', password='secret', return_node=True)
>>> pp(node.enable('show version'))
[{'command': 'show version',
  'encoding': 'json',
  'result': {u'architecture': u'i386',
             u'bootupTimestamp': 1421765066.11,
             u'hardwareRevision': u'',
             u'internalBuildId': u'f590eed4-1e66-43c6-8943-cee0390fbafe',
             u'internalVersion': u'4.14.5F-2209869.4145F',
             u'memFree': 115496,
             u'memTotal': 2028008,
             u'modelName': u'vEOS',
             u'serialNumber': u'',
             u'systemMacAddress': u'00:0c:29:f5:d2:7d',
             u'version': u'4.14.5F'}}]
```

Looking at both Cisco and Arista (which are two major players in the cloud and SDN marketplace), we can combine both Arista eAPI and Cisco NX-API to manage our entire data center inventory, and work on some tasks like the provisioning of new devices or upgrading of current devices with no or minimal impact, which in turn ensures scalability, reliability, and uptime in the business processes.

Controller-based network fabric

As we come out of the legacy hardware era in which each physical path was connected and designed to take traffic from one point to another, and where a packet had limited availability to reach from one device to another, SDN is ensuring that we have a network fabric for our data to reach between different sources and destinations.

A **network fabric** is a collection of different network devices connected to each other by a common controller ensuring that each component in the network is optimized to send traffic among each of the nodes. The underlying switch fabric, which is a physical switchboard with ports (like Ethernet, ATM, and DSL), is also controlled and programmed by a controller which can ensure (by creating a path or specific port(s)) that a particular type of data can traverse through to reach its destinations.

In a typical network design we have Layer 2 (or switching domains) and Layer 3 (or routing domains). If we do not have a controller-based approach, each network component can learn the behavior of traffic from its next connected component (like **Spanning Tree Protocol** (**STP**) for Layer 2) or some routing protocol (like OSPF for Layer 3). In this case, each device acts as its own controller and only has limited visibility to devices that it is directly connected to (also termed **neighbor devices**). There is no single view of the entire network on any device, and additionally, each component (or individual controller) acts as a single point of failure for its neighbor devices. A failure on any component would result in its neighbor devices re converging or even getting isolated owing to the failure of their connected component.

Comparing that to a controller-based environment, theoretically each device has as many connections as it has number of ports connected. Hence, if we think of even three devices connected in a controller-based environment, we have multiple connections between each device owing to their physical connectivity to each other. In case of the failure of a component (or device), the controller can quickly make an intelligent decision to reconfigure a new path and alter the behavior of the other two network devices to ensure minimal disruption to traffic, keeping the same throughput and distributed load on all the other available links. A controller in theory eliminates the control plane behavior of each device and ensures an optimized forwarding table (to forward data to specific destinations) is updated on each device the controller is managing. This is because the controller starts acting as the main component which has the visibility of every device, with every entry and exit point of each device and the granularity of the data type that is flowing from each managed network device.

Going by the vendors, major players such as Cisco (with its open network environment), Juniper (with its QFabric switch), and Avaya (with its VENA switch), have provided the ability to act as controllers or be configured to be managed by a controller. Additionally, with the introduction of controller-to-manager network components, each network device can now virtually become a dump client with the controller making all the intelligent decisions, from learning to forwarding tables.

A controller acts as an abstraction layer between multi-vendor network devices and network tasks. As an end user, someone can configure specific tasks to be performed by the controller, and, using the underlying API model from different vendors (using JSON or XML), the controller can convert those specific tasks into various vendor-specific API calls, and devices can be configured by sending those specific instructions using those APIs to each of the vendor devices. The **Application Policy Infrastructure Controller (APIC)** component is responsible for controlling and programming the fabric on each network device component.

Let's see an example of Cisco APIC and some basics on how we can use it. Cisco APIC is used to manage, automate, monitor, and program **Application Centric Infrastructure (ACI)**. ACI is a collection of objects with each object representing a tenant. A tenant can be called a group of specific customers, groups, or business units based upon the business classifications. As an example, a single organization may covert its entire infrastructure into a single tenant, whereas an organization can separate out its tenants based upon its functions like HR and Finance. Tenants can further be divided into contexts, with each context as a separate forwarding plane, hence the same set of IP addresses can be used in each context as each set of IP addresses will be treated differently in each context.

Contexts contain **Endpoints (EPs)** and **Endpoint Groups (EPGs)**. These EPs are physical components like hardware NICs, and EPGs are collections of items like DNSs, IP addresses, and so on, that dictate a similar functionality for a specific application (like a web application).

For programming with APIC, the major components required are as follows:

- **APIC Rest Python Adaptor (ARYA)**

    This is a tool created by Cisco to convert the APIC object returned in XML or JSON to direct Python code. Underlying, this leverages the COBRA SDK to perform this task. This can be installed in Python using `pip install arya`.

- **ACI SDK**

    This is the SDK that contains the API to directly call the APIs of the controller. We need to install `acicobra`, which can be found at `https://www.cisco.com/c/en/us/td/docs/switches/datacenter/aci/apic/sw/1-x/api/python/install/b_Install_Cisco_APIC_Python_SDK_Standalone.html`, from Cisco to be able to call it into Python.

Once we have this installed, here are some examples from Cisco which can be found at the URL https://github.com/CiscoDevNet/python_code_samples_network/blob/master/ acitoolkit_show_tenants/aci-show-tenants.py. This can help us understand creating an object:

```python
#!/usr/bin/env python
"""
Simple application that logs on to the APIC and displays all
of the Tenants.
Leverages the DevNet Sandbox - APIC Simulator Always On
    Information at
https://developer.cisco.com/site/devnet/sandbox/available-labs/data-center/
index.gsp
Code sample based off the ACI-Toolkit Code sample
https://github.com/datacenter/acitoolkit/blob/master/samples/aci-show-tenan
ts.py
"""

import sys
import acitoolkit.acitoolkit as ACI

# Credentials and information for the DevNet ACI Simulator Always-On
Sandbox
APIC_URL = "https://sandboxapicdc.cisco.com/"
APIC_USER = "admin"
APIC_PASSWORD = "C1sco12345"

def main():
    """
    Main execution routine
    :return: None
    """

    # Login to APIC
    session = ACI.Session(APIC_URL, APIC_USER, APIC_PASSWORD)
    resp = session.login()
    if not resp.ok:
        print('%% Could not login to APIC')
        sys.exit(0)

    # Download all of the tenants
    print("TENANT")
    print("------")
    tenants = ACI.Tenant.get(session)
    for tenant in tenants:
        print(tenant.name)
```

```
if __name__ == '__main__':
    main()
```

Looking at the preceding concepts, we can enhance and ensure that our managed nodes in the controller can be controlled based on the application requirements rather than hardware limitations. This also ensures that the infrastructure is now tweaked as per application, and not vice versa, with the application performance restricted by hardware.

Network automation tools

As we have seen throughout the previous chapters, we have multiple choices regarding automating a network. From a basic configuration for any device using Netmiko to deploying and creating configurations across various devices in a network using Ansible, there are many options for engineers to automate networks based upon various needs.

Python is extensively used in creating automation scenarios, owing to its open community support for various vendors and protocols. Nearly every major player in the industry has support for Python programming, tweaking their own tools or any supporting technology that they have. Another major aspect of network automation are the custom-based solutions that could be made for organization requirements. The self-service API model is a good start to ensuring that some of the tasks that are done manually can be converted to APIs, which can then be leveraged into any language based upon the automation needs.

Let's see an example that can be used as a basic guide to understand the advantage of self or custom-created automation tools. The output of `show ip bgp summary` in Cisco is the same as `show bgp summary` in Juniper. Now, as an engineer who needs to validate the BGP on both the vendors, I need to understand both the commands and interpret the output.

Think of this situation by adding more vendors which have their own unique way of fetching BGP output. This becomes complex and a network engineer needs to be trained on a multi-vendor environment to be able to fetch the same type of output from each vendor.

Now, let's say we create an API (for example, `getbgpstatus`), which takes the input as some hostname. The API at the backend is intelligent enough to fetch the vendor model using SNMP, and based upon the vendor sends a specific command (like `show ip bgp summary` for Cisco or `show ip summary` for Juniper), and parses that output to a human-readable format, like only the IP address and status of that BGP neighbor.

For example, instead of printing the raw output of `show ip bgp summary` or `show bgp summary`, it parses the output like this:

```
IPaddress1 : Status is UP
IPaddress2 : Status is Down (Active)
```

This output can be returned as a JSON value back to the call of the API.

Hence, let's say we can call the API as `http://localhost/networkdevices/getbgpstatus?device=devicex` and the API from the backend will identify if `devicex` is Juniper or Cisco or any other vendor, and based upon this the vendor will fetch and parse the output relevant to that vendor. A return of that API call will be JSON text as we saw in the preceding example, that we can parse in our automation language.

Let us see a basic example of another popular tool, SolarWinds. There are many aspects of SolarWinds; it can auto-discover a device (based upon MIBs and SNMP), identify the vendor, and fetch relevant information from the device.

Let's see some of the following screenshots for basic SolarWinds device management. SolarWinds is freely available as a trial download.

The prerequisite for SolarWinds device management is as follows:

1. We need to add a device in SolarWinds, shown as below:

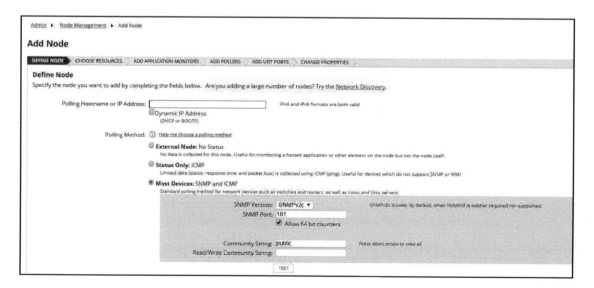

As we can see, SolarWinds has the ability to discover devices (using network discovery), or we can add a specific IP address/hostname with the correct SNMP string for SolarWinds to detect the device.

2. Once the device is detected it will show as the monitored node, as in the below screenshot:

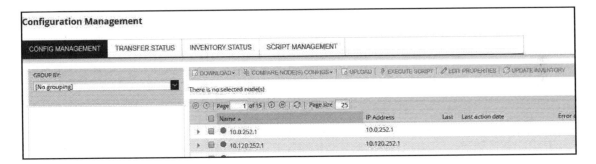

Notice the green dot next to the IP address (or hostname). This signifies that the node is alive (reachable) and SolarWinds can interact with the node correctly.

Additional task(s) that can be performed post device discovery is as follows:

Once we have the node available or detected in SolarWinds, here are some of the additional tasks that can be performed in SolarWinds (as shown in screenshot below):

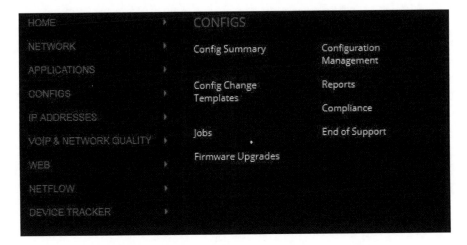

We have selected the **CONFIGS** menu, under which we can perform config management for the devices. Additionally, as we can see in the following screenshot, we have the ability to create small scripts, (like we did here to `show running config`), which we can use to execute against a certain set of devices from SolarWinds itself (as in screenshot below):

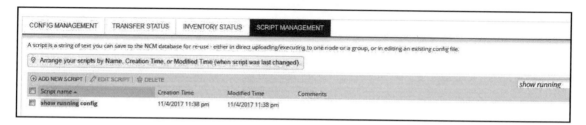

The result is retrieved and can be stored as a text file, or can even be sent as a report back to any email client if configured. Similarly, there are certain tasks (called **jobs** in SolarWinds), that can be done on a scheduled basis, as we can see in the following screenshot:

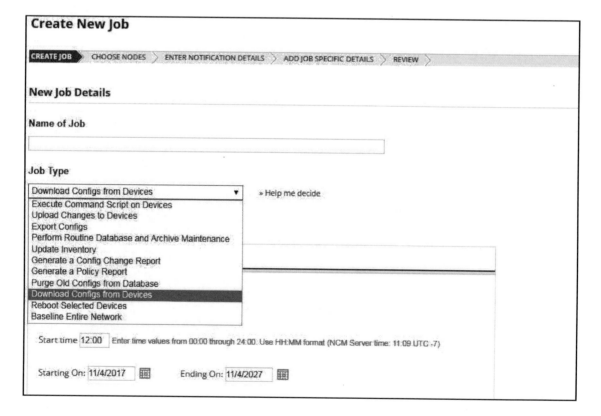

As we can see in the preceding screenshot, we can **Download Configs from Devices**, and then select all or certain devices in the next step and schedule the job. This is very useful in terms of fetching a config from a previous date or in case a rollback is needed to a last known good config scenario. Also, there are times when auditing needs to be performed regarding who changed what and what was changed in configurations, and SolarWinds can extend this ability by sending reports and alerts. Programmatically, we have the additional ability to call the SolarWinds API to fetch the results from Python.

 It is assumed that OrionSDK is already installed in Python. If not, we can install it using `pip install orionsdk`.

Consider the following example:

```python
from orionsdk import SwisClient
import requests

npm_server = 'myserver'
username = "username"
password = "password"

verify = False
if not verify:
    from requests.packages.urllib3.exceptions import InsecureRequestWarning
    requests.packages.urllib3.disable_warnings(InsecureRequestWarning)

swis = SwisClient(npm_server, username, password)

results = swis.query("SELECT NodeID, DisplayName FROM Orion.Nodes Where Vendor= 'Cisco'")

for row in results['results']:
    print("{NodeID:<5}: {DisplayName}".format(**row))
```

Since SolarWinds supports a direct SQL query, we use the query:

```
SELECT NodeID, DisplayName FROM Orion.Nodes Where Vendor= 'Cisco'
```

We are trying to fetch the `NodeID` and `DisplayName` (or the device name) for all the devices which have the vendor Cisco. Once we have the result, we print the result in a formatted way. In our case, the output will be (let's assume our Cisco devices in SolarWinds are added as `mytestrouter1` and `mytestrouter2`):

```
>>>
===================== RESTART: C:\a1\checksolarwinds.py
=====================
101 : mytestrouter1
102 : mytestrouter2
>>>
```

Using some of these automation tools and APIs, we can ensure that our tasks are focused on actual work with some of the basic or core tasks (like fetching values from devices and so on) being offloaded to the tools or APIs to take care of.

Let's now create a basic automation tool from scratch that monitors the reachability of any node that is part of that monitoring tool, using a ping test. We can call it PingMesh or PingMatrix, as the tool will generate a web-based matrix to show the reachability of the routers.

The topology that we would be using is as follows:

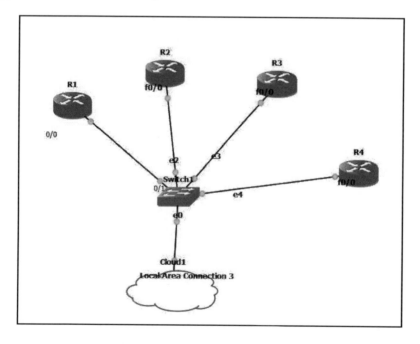

Here, we would be using four routers (R1 to R4), and the Cloud1 as our monitoring source. Each of the routers will try to reach each other through ping, and will report back to the script running on Cloud1 which will interpret the results and display the web-based matrix through a web-based URL.

The explanation of the preceding topology is as follows:

1. What we are trying to do is log in to each router (preferably in parallel), ping each destination from each source, and report back the reachability status of each destination.
2. As an example, if we want to do the task manually, we would log in to R1 and try to ping R2, R3, and R4 from the source to check the reachability of each router from R1. The main script on Cloud1 (acting as the controller) will interpret the result and update the web matrix accordingly.
3. In our case all the routers (and the controller) are residing in 192.168.255.x subnet, hence they are reachable to each other using a simple ping.

We are going to create two separate Python programs (one to be called as the library for invoking the commands on various nodes, fetching the results from the nodes, interpreting the results, and sending the parsed data to the main program). The main program will be responsible for calling the library, and will use the results we get back to create the HTML web matrix.

Let's create the library or the program to be called in the main program first (we called it getmeshvalues.py):

```python
#!/usr/bin/env python
import re
import sys
import os
import time
from netmiko import ConnectHandler
from threading import Thread
from random import randrange
username="cisco"
password="cisco"

splitlist = lambda lst, sz: [lst[i:i+sz] for i in range(0, len(lst), sz)]

returns = {}
resultoutput={}
devlist=[]
cmdlist=""
def fetchallvalues(sourceip,sourcelist,delay,cmddelay):
```

```
        print ("checking for....."+sourceip)
        cmdend=" repeat 10" # this is to ensure that we ping for 10 packets
        splitsublist=splitlist(sourcelist,6) # this is to ensure we open not
more than 6 sessions on router at a time
        threads_imagex= []
        for item in splitsublist:
            t = Thread(target=fetchpingvalues,
args=(sourceip,item,cmdend,delay,cmddelay,))
            t.start()
            time.sleep(randrange(1,2,1)/20)
            threads_imagex.append(t)


        for t in threads_imagex:
            t.join()
def fetchpingvalues(devip,destips,cmdend,delay,cmddelay):
    global resultoutput
    ttl="0"
    destip="none"
    command=""
    try:
        output=""
        device = ConnectHandler(device_type='cisco_ios', ip=devip,
username=username, password=password, global_delay_factor=cmddelay)
        time.sleep(delay)
        device.clear_buffer()
        for destip in destips:
            command="ping "+destip+" source "+devip+cmdend
            output =
device.send_command_timing(command,delay_factor=cmddelay)
            if ("round-trip" in output):
                resultoutput[devip+":"+destip]="True"
            elif ("Success rate is 0 percent" in output):
                resultoutput[devip+":"+destip]="False"
        device.disconnect()
    except:
        print ("Error connecting to ..."+devip)
        for destip in destips:
            resultoutput[devip+":"+destip]="False"

def getallvalues(allips):
    global resultoutput
    threads_imagex= []
    for item in allips:
        #print ("calling "+item)
        t = Thread(target=fetchallvalues, args=(item,allips,2,1,))
        t.start()
        time.sleep(randrange(1,2,1)/30)
        threads_imagex.append(t)
```

```
    for t in threads_imagex:
        t.join()
    dnew=sorted(resultoutput.items())
    return dnew

#print
(getallvalues(["192.168.255.240","192.168.255.245","192.168.255.248","192.1
68.255.249","4.2.2.2"]))
```

In the preceding code, we have created three main functions that we call in a thread (for parallel execution). The `getallvalues()` contains the list of IP addresses that we want to get the data from. It then passes this information to `fetchallvalues()` with specific device information to fetch the ping values again in parallel execution. For executing the command on the router and fetching the results, we call the `fetchpingvalues()` function.

Let's see the result of this code (by removing the remark on the code that calls the function). We need to pass the device IPs that we want to validate as a list. In our case, we have all the valid routers in the `192.168.255.x` range, and `4.2.2.2` is taken as an example of a non-reachable router:

```
print(getallvalues(["192.168.255.240","192.168.255.245","192.168.255.248","
192.168.255.249","4.2.2.2"]))
```

The preceding code gives the following output:

As we can see in the result, we get the reachability in terms of `True` or `False` from each node to the other node.

For example, the first item in the list (`'192.168.255.240:192.168.255.240'`, `'True'`) interprets that from the source `192.168.255.240` to destination `192.168.255.240` (which is the same self IP) is reachable. Similarly, the next item in the same list (`'192.168.255.240:192.168.255.245'`, `'True'`) confirms that from source IP `192.168.255.240` the destination `192.168.255.245` we have reachability from ping. This information is required to create a matrix based upon the results. Next we see the main code where we fetch these results and create a web-based matrix page.

Next, we need to create the main file (we're calling it `pingmesh.py`):

```python
import getmeshvalue
from getmeshvalue import getallvalues

getdevinformation={}
devicenamemapping={}
arraydeviceglobal=[]
pingmeshvalues={}

arraydeviceglobal=["192.168.255.240","192.168.255.245","192.168.255.248","192.168.255.249","4.2.2.2"]

devicenamemapping['192.168.255.240']="R1"
devicenamemapping['192.168.255.245']="R2"
devicenamemapping['192.168.255.248']="R3"
devicenamemapping['192.168.255.249']="R4"
devicenamemapping['4.2.2.2']="Random"

def getmeshvalues():
        global arraydeviceglobal
        global pingmeshvalues
        arraydeviceglobal=sorted(set(arraydeviceglobal))
        tval=getallvalues(arraydeviceglobal)
        pingmeshvalues = dict(tval)

getmeshvalues()

def createhtml():
    global arraydeviceglobal
    fopen=open("C:\pingmesh\pingmesh.html","w")  ### this needs to be
changed as web path of the html location

    head="""<html><head><meta http-equiv="refresh" content="60" ></head>"""
```

```
        head=head+"""<script type="text/javascript">
function updatetime() {
    var x = new Date(document.lastModified);
    document.getElementById("modified").innerHTML = "Last Modified: "+x+"
";
}
</script>"""+"<body onLoad='updatetime();'>"
    head=head+"<div style='display: inline-block;float: right;font-size:
80%'><h4><h4><p id='modified'></p></div>"
    head=head+"<div style='display: inline-block;float: left;font-size:
90%'></h4><center><h2>Network Health Dashboard<h2></div>"
    head=head+"<br><div><table border='1' align='center'><caption><b>Ping
Matrix</b></caption>"
    head=head+"<center><br><br><br><br><br><br><br><br>"
    fopen.write(head)
    dval=""
    fopen.write("<tr><td>Devices</td>")
    for fromdevice in arraydeviceglobal:
        fopen.write("<td><b>"+devicenamemapping[fromdevice]+"</b></td>")
    fopen.write("</tr>")
    for fromdevice in arraydeviceglobal:
        fopen.write("<tr>")
        fopen.write("<td><b>"+devicenamemapping[fromdevice]+"</b></td>")
        for todevice in arraydeviceglobal:
            askvalue=fromdevice+":"+todevice
            if (askvalue in pingmeshvalues):
                getallvalues=pingmeshvalues.get(askvalue)
                bgcolor='lime'
                if (getallvalues == "False"):
                    bgcolor='salmon'
            fopen.write("<td align='center' font size='2' height='2'
width='2' bgcolor='"+bgcolor+"'title='"+askvalue+"'>"+"<font
color='white'><b>"+getallvalues+"</b></font></td>")
        fopen.write("</tr>\n")
    fopen.write("</table></div>")
    fopen.close()
createhtml()


print("All done!!!!")
```

In this case, we have the following mappings in place:

```
devicenamemapping['192.168.255.240']="R1"
devicenamemapping['192.168.255.245']="R2"
devicenamemapping['192.168.255.248']="R3"
devicenamemapping['192.168.255.249']="R4"
devicenamemapping['4.2.2.2']="Random"
```

The last device named `Random`, is a test device which is not in our network and is non-reachable for test purposes. Once executed, it creates a file named `pingmesh.html` with standard HTML formats and a last-refreshed clock (from JavaScript) to confirm when the last refresh occurred. This is required if we want the script to be executed from the task scheduler (Let's say every five minutes), and anybody opening the HTML page will know when the probe occurred. The HTML file needs to be placed or saved in a folder which is mapped to a web folder so that it can be accessed using the URL `http://<server>/pingmesh.html`.

When executed, here is the output from the Python script:

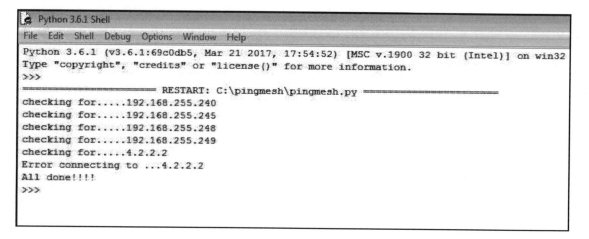

The HTML file, when placed in the web-mapped URL and called, looks like this:

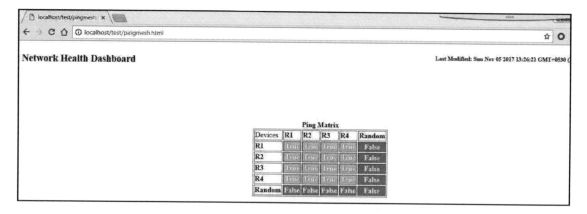

As we can see, in the PingMatrix there is an entire red row and column, which means that any connectivity between any router to the random router and from the random router to any router is not there. Green means that all the connectivity between all other routers is fine.

Additionally, we have also configured a tooltip on each cell, and hovering the mouse over that specific cell would also show the source and destination IP address mapping for that particular cell, as shown in the following screenshot:

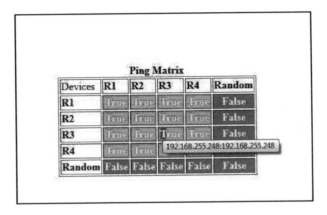

Let's see another screenshot, in which we shut down R2 to make it unreachable:

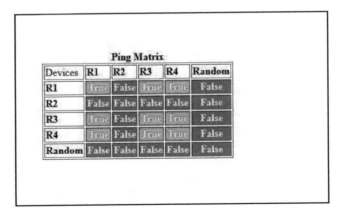

Now, as we can see, the entire row and column of R2 is red, and hence the PingMatrix shows that R2 is now unreachable from everywhere else, and R2 also cannot reach anyone else in the network.

Let's see a final example, in which for test purposes we intentionally block the ping traffic from R2 to R4 (and vice versa) using an extended Cisco ACL, which in turn reports that R4 and R2 have reachability issues in the PingMatrix:

Ping Matrix

Devices	R1	R2	R3	R4	Random
R1	True	True	True	True	False
R2	True	True	True	False	False
R3	True	True	True	True	False
R4	True	False	True	True	False
Random	False	Fa 192.168.255.249:192.168.255.245			

As we see can in the preceding screenshot, the Random router is still a red or false, since it is not in our network, but now it is showing red/false between R2 and R4 and also between R4 and R2. This gives us a quick view that even with multiple paths to reach each node with another node, we have a connectivity issue between the two nodes.

Going by the preceding examples, we can enhance the tool to easily monitor and understand any routing/reachability issues, or even link down connectivity problems using a holistic view of all of the connections in our network. PingMesh/Matrix can be extended to check latency, and even packet drops in each connection between various nodes. Additionally, using syslog or email functionality (specific Python libraries are available for sending syslog messages from Python or even emails from Python code), alerts or tickets can also be generated in case of failures detected or high latency observed from the Python script itself.

This tool can easily become a central monitoring tool in any organization, and based upon patterns (such as green or red, and other color codes if needed), engineers can make decisions on the actual issues and take proactive actions instead of reactive actions to ensure the high reliability and uptime of the network.

Summary

In this chapter, we learned about the basic functionality of SDN controllers, programmable fabric, and some network automation tools. We have also seen how to work with cloud platforms and, with reference to a live example of managing AWS Cloud from Python, understood how we can control cloud operations using automation.

We gained a deep understanding about the role of controllers, and with some examples of Cisco controllers, went into details on how a controller can be programmed or called in programs/scripts to perform certain tasks. We also saw the basics of some popular network automation tools, such as SolarWinds, and created an in-house web-based automation tool for monitoring our network, called PingMatrix or PingMesh.

Index

Made in the USA
San Bernardino, CA
17 July 2018